DISCARD

Bosnia and Herzegovina

MICHAEL A. SCHUMAN

☑®

Facts On File, Inc.

949.742 SCH

Schuman, Michael.
Bosnia and Herzegovina.

Nations in Transition: Bosnia and Herzegovina

Copyright © 2004 by Michael A. Schuman

All rights reserved. No part of this book may be reproduced or utilized in any form or by any means, electronic or mechanical, including photocopying, recording, or by any information storage or retrieval systems, without permission in writing from the publisher. For information contact:

Facts On File, Inc.
132 West 31st Street
New York NY 10001

Library of Congress Cataloging-in-Publication Data

Schuman, Michael.
   Bosnia and Herzegovina / Michael Schuman.
      p. cm. — (Nations in transition)
   Includes bibliographical references and index.
   ISBN 0-8160-5052-X (alk. paper)
   1. Bosnia and Herzegovina. I. Title. II. Series.

DR1660.S38 2003
949.742—dc21   2003045870

Facts On File books are available at special discounts when purchased in bulk quantities for businesses, associations, institutions, or sales promotions. Please call our Special Sales Department in New York at (212) 967-8800 or (800) 322-8755.

You can find Facts On File on the World Wide Web at
http://www.factsonfile.com

Text design by Erika K. Arroyo
Cover design by Nora Wertz
Maps by Patricia Meschino © Facts On File

Printed in the United States of America

MP FOF 10 9 8 7 6 5 4 3 2 1

This book is printed on acid-free paper.

AMITY HIGH SCHOOL LIBRARY
WOODBRIDGE CT 06525
86008392

CONTENTS

BOSNIA-HERZEGOVINA

0   50 miles
0   50 km

Bosanski
Brod

Bosanski
Šamac

Brčko

Una R.

Sana R. • Prijedor

Derventa

• Bihać

Sanski Most

Doboj

Bijeljina

Bosanski
Petrovac

• Banja Luka

Tuzla

Vrbas R.

Serbia

Ključ

Bosna R. • Banovići

• Drvar

Jajce

Travnik

Zenica

Kladanj

Svornik

• Bosansko
Grahovo

Vitez

Srebrenica

CROATIA

• Glamoč

Gornji Vakuf

Žepa

Livno

Sarajevo ✪

Pale

Višegrad

Drina R.

Goražde

Foča

Neretva R.

Kalinovik

Mostar

Vitina

• Ljubuški

Gacko

SERBIA AND MONTENEGRO

Stolac

Neum

Montenegro

Trebinje

Adriatic Sea

N

Federation of
Bosnia and Herzegovina

Republika Srpska
(Serb Republic)

Republic borders

o   Under international
     supervision

INTRODUCTION

Mention the name *Bosnia* to anyone who followed the news in the early 1990s and he or she will likely reply with one comment: "Oh, that's where the war was."

From 1992 through 1995 this small corner of Europe was the scene of a horrible war that produced some of the continent's worst carnage of the late 20th century. To understand this conflict it is helpful to know something about the history of Bosnia.

The full name of the nation is Republic of Bosnia and Herzegovina, sometimes shortened to Bosnia-Herzegovina. In the local language, the name of the country is abbreviated as BiH. Because the name is cumbersome to write and pronounce, many simply abbreviate it as Bosnia. In this book I will use the names *Bosnia* and *Bosnia and Herzegovina* interchangeably.

The country is named for two separate areas. Bosnia is a mountainous region of the Balkan Peninsula in southeastern Europe, and Herzegovina is a smaller area south of Bosnia. Together they are one country. Until 1991 Bosnia and Herzegovina was part of Yugoslavia.

Located not far from the point where Europe meets Asia, Bosnia and Herzegovina has been ruled by many different peoples over the centuries, including Turks, Austrians, and Serbs. Put another way, Bosnia has been under the thumb of many cultures and religions, including Catholics, Orthodox Christians, Muslims, and a government that was officially atheistic.

As a result of this past, Bosnia and Herzegovina is a true mosaic of cultures. One can see evidence of this while traveling the country or even walking down the streets of the nation's capital, Sarajevo. Mosques and Turkish marketplaces are neighbors with Christian churches and Jewish synagogues. Although the Jews never governed Bosnia and Herzegovina, there has been a Jewish presence there for centuries.

HOW TO SPEAK SERBO-CROATIAN

Most of the letters in the Latin alphabet are pronounced the same as in English. There are exceptions, however. The letter *j* is pronounced like the consonant *y,* as in *yellow.* The letters *lj* together sound like the *lli* in *billion.* Along those lines, *nj* is voiced like the *ny* together in *canyon.* The letter *š* (with a haček [or *kavaca* in Serbo-Croatian] above it) takes the sound of "sh." If you are planning to write the letter *c,* be careful. A plain *c* with no mark above it sounds like "ts," as in *hats.* A *ć* (with an acute accent above it) takes on the "tch sound," as in *itch.* A *č* (with a haček atop it) is spoken like the "ch" sound as in *chair.*

Serbo-Croatian family names have suffixes, prefixes, and patterns just like English ones. The vast majority end in *ić,* pronounced "itch" and meaning "child of," similar to the suffix *son* in English. One will also notice that women's first names almost always end in *a* or *ica,* pronounced "eet-sa."

This mosaic of cultures has made Bosnia and Herzegovina a fascinating place, and there have been long periods in which they coexisted peacefully. However, this history of changing rulers also explains the country's numerous wars and endless civil unrest. Among the people of Bosnia and Herzegovina are native Muslims, known today as Bosniaks. Others are Serbs who practice the Eastern Orthodox branch of Christianity. There is also a sizable population of Croatian Catholics, and a significant minority of Jews living mainly in the cities.

Many people wonder who should run Bosnia and Herzegovina. If Bosniaks make the rules, will Serbs be treated unfairly? If the Serbs run the government and most private businesses, will the Croats suffer? These are the questions that make for a permanent uneasiness among Bosnia's citizens.

While these issues dominate the makeup of nearly every country in the world, including the United States, differences among Bosniaks, Serbs, and Croats are deeply rooted, reaching back nearly 1,000 years, as you will see.

Bosnian society is complex to the point of having two different official alphabets—Latin and Cyrillic. And although people here speak the same language, the country is known among the residents by three different names, depending on their nationality. The official language is Serbo-Croatian. However, Bosniaks refer to it as Bosnian; Serbs call it Serbian; and Croats identify it as Croatian. All this variety is found in a nation of only 3.9 million people.

Geography

With an area of 51,129 square kilometers (19,741 square miles), Bosnia and Herzegovina is a bit smaller in size than West Virginia. To put it in European terms, Bosnia and Herzegovina comprises about one-tenth the area of France. If you are looking for breathtaking vistas, Bosnia and Herzegovina is the country to visit. The craggy mountain range known as the Dinaric Alps is filled with dense thickets of forest and dominates northern Bosnia. The land in this high elevation is used mainly for cattle farming and fruit growing. The southern stretches of the nation, mostly in the region of Herzegovina, have rugged hills and flat plains, good for harvesting a variety of crops. Bosnia has a tiny coastline along the Adriatic Sea, measuring just 20 kilometers, or approximately 12.5 miles. The country's elevation ranges from sea level to 2,386 meters (7,828 feet).

There are several rivers in Bosnia and Herzegovina, but the main one is the Sava, which forms the border between Bosnia and Croatia to the north. The Sava has several tributaries that—appropriately enough for this unusual country—flow from south to north instead of the expected direction of north to south. These include the Bosna, Vrbas, Una, and Drina. Only one important river, the Neretva, flows north to south, emptying in the Adriatic Sea.

The towns in and around the mountains contend with cold and snowy winters and warm but rainy summers. In Herzegovina winters are mild and rainy while summers are mainly hot and dry.

Bosnia and Herzegovina shares boundaries with just two countries. To the northeast it abuts the Yugoslav republic of Serbia, while to the southeast it borders the Yugoslav republic of Montenegro (together the two republics make up the present-day nation known as Serbia and Montenegro). With the exception of the tiny stretch of Adriatic Sea coastline, the rest of Bosnia and Herzegovina borders Croatia, which was once also a Yugoslavian republic but is now an independent nation. Croatia surrounds Bosnia and Herzegovina like the thumb and forefinger of a hand; a thin stretch of Croatian land separates Bosnia and Herzegovina from most of the Adriatic Sea.

In general, Bosnia and Herzegovina looks like a rough triangle. And that is the basic emblem on the nation's flag: a yellow triangle, in the middle of a blue field, is bordered by nine white stars. The stars are designed so that just the bottom half of the top star and the top half of the bottom star show—as if the stars are stretching off the flag into infinity.

The flag's ultra-modern design has lent itself to many interpretations, but basically it is meant to be neutral, so as not to show favoritism toward one of Bosnia's ethnic groups over another. The line of stars is said to represent the endless heavens. Whether the nation can live up to the ideals presented in its flag remains to be seen.

PART I
History

1

From Prehistory to the Assassination of Archduke Francis Ferdinand

If one traveled 3,000 years back in time to the country known today as Bosnia and Herzegovina, one would see a mountainous but mostly uninhabited land, with rushing rivers and deep woods. Gradually, groups of warriors from other parts of Europe and Asia would enter the region to make homes of wood or mud and live together in tribes and clans. And so the long human history of this fascinating part of the world would begin.

Today we call these ancient people Illyrians, and their land Illyria. For more than 1,000 years they worked, played, worshiped, and chose governments just like any other civilization. The Illyrians earned their living by growing grains, by hunting and fishing, and by raising and trading cattle and horses with other tribes. They also made and traded tools, weapons, and ornaments crafted from copper and iron, and crafted basic pottery and textiles.

The various tribes were governed by chiefs selected by bodies called councils of elders. Now and then the Illyrians set up kingdoms, but none lasted long. Thanks to the existence of age-old friezes found in the area, we know that the Illyrians often pirated and made war on their neighbors.

■ 3 ■

By the year 400 B.C. the Greek Empire was thriving, and Greek leaders Philip II of Macedonia (382–336 B.C.) and his son, Alexander the Great (356–323 B.C.), both made inroads into Illyria. During the next century Celts invaded the land. Both the Greeks and Celts left cultural influences in Illyria. Then, in attacks which took place in 229 and 168 B.C., the powerful Roman Empire invaded and conquered much of Illyria. In A.D. 9, Illyria became an official Roman province called Illyricum. The Romans built temples, coliseums, public baths, and an intricate roadway system. The Roman Empire was divided in A.D. 395 into western and eastern sections, each of which eventually had its own language, culture, and religion. The border between the two empires cut through Bosnia along the Drina River. The Western Roman Empire fell in 476 to invading barbarians (a collective term for many Germanic peoples) while the Eastern Roman Empire, with its capital in Constantinople (ancient Byzantium, later Istanbul, Turkey), became the Byzantine Empire.

Charlemagne, leader of the Franks, conquered the Slavs in the eighth century in what is now present-day Bosnia. (Courtesy Free Library of Philadelphia)

New Arrivals

As the Roman Empire began to crumble in the 500s, a group of tribesmen called the Slavs began filtering from the northeast into what is now Bosnia. There are few written records of their lives, but it is believed that they governed themselves peacefully for about a century. Then in the mid- and late 600s, other Slavic tribal groups entered the region. The Croats came from the north and from the south and east came the Serbs. Like the earlier settlers, they lived in small tribal units. All three groups belonged to the same ethnic group, a large confederation called the Slaveni.

Conflict was common over the next few hundred years. In the late 700s, the Franks, tribes from present-day Germany and France, conquered the Slavs of present-day Bosnia. Under the famous Frankish Charlemagne (768–814), many Slavs became serfs: members of a servile class of people who were owned by a lord and obligated to his orders. They were also forced to renounce their pagan belief in many gods and

Some of the more unusual art of medieval Bosnia is expressed in the stećci, more than 60,000 tombstones found throughout Sarajevo. At one time it was thought that only Bogomils were buried under the stećci, but it is now believed that Orthodox and Catholic Christians used them to mark the resting places of their dead too. (AP/Wide World Photos)

become Christians. In the 900s, these early Slavs were then conquered in rapid succession by kingdoms of Serbs, Croatians, and Bulgarians.

In the early 1000s, the Byzantine Empire defeated and took control over Bulgaria, including the Slavs of Bosnia. The Byzantines practiced a form of Christianity different from Catholicism called Eastern Orthodox. (This will be explained further in the chapter on religion.)

In 1137 the kingdom of Hungary to the north seized control of almost all of Bosnia, only to lose it again to the Byzantine Empire in 1167. The Byzantines held Bosnia for just 13 years, until 1180, when Hungary again snatched Bosnia. Hungary ran Bosnia as a suzerain, meaning Hungary controlled Bosnia's relations with other nations but allowed it to govern its own internal affairs.

A New Religion

In 1180, Bosnia's king, called by the title *ban*, was named Kulin. Eager to establish Bosnian independence, he rejected the standard forms of Christianity of the time—Catholic or Orthodox. He decreed that Bosnians would follow the medieval Christian sect called Bogomilism. Historians believe that Bogomilism probably caught on because the Bosnians and their immediate Balkan neighbors wanted independence from the powerful Catholics to the west and the Orthodox Christians to the east.

King Kulin's reign, from 1180 to 1204, marked a wonderful period of peace in Bosnian history. Sometime during Kulin's reign Bosnia became an independent kingdom, separate from Hungarian rule. This period is referred to as the "golden age of Kulin Ban."

However, to both Catholics and Orthodox Christians, Bogomils were heretics who needed to be set straight. Kulin Ban was eventually tortured by Hungarian Catholics until he renounced Bogomilism. Regardless, other Bosnians continued to practice Bogomilism for some time.

Frustrated, Pope Gregory IX (1145–1241) declared a crusade, or holy war, sending Hungarian Catholics to invade Bosnia several times between 1235 and 1241. They penetrated Bosnia as far south as Sarajevo (then called Vrhbosna) but were forced to withdraw. After rejecting further attempts from the pope to control them, the Bosnians ultimately separated themselves from the Catholic Church. They set up their own

BOGOMILISM

Bogomilism is a Christian denomination that is hardly heard of today: In fact, it no longer has any practitioners. But at one time Bogomilism was the religion of much of the Balkan region of Europe. How it started is a mystery. Some historians say it was named after a priest named Bogomil who lived in Macedonia, a district of the Balkans south of Bosnia, in the 900s. Others believe the name comes from two words in the Bulgarian language: *Bog* for God and *mil* for friend.

Bogomilism was considered a "dualist" religion. Bogomils rejected the Catholic claim that the world was inherently evil, asserting instead that there were two gods: one who was evil and one who was good. Satan, or Satanael, was a rebel son of God who created the human body and material wealth whereas the god of good created the human soul. Poverty was viewed as a virtue. Material possessions and their owners were considered evil. When Bogomilism emerged, Macedonia was controlled by its bigger neighbor, Bulgaria, and was populated by mostly poor villagers, many of whom labored resentfully as serfs for Bulgarian landowners. Obviously, Bogomilism was as much of a social movement as it was a religion.

The Bogomils rejected material forms of Christianity, including churches, crucifixes, and other religious icons. They prayed to Jesus in their homes and did not recognize bishops as authorities; bishops were seen as false teachers. In fact, Bogomils went so far as to reward rebellion against authorities, especially the military and those who exploited the poor. At home, they practiced sexual abstinence and avoided wine and meat.

Even without that, Bogomilism thrived among the Slavs for some time because, it is believed, it was the only religion with Slavic origins. Bogomilism then spread from Macedonia into Bulgaria and Bosnia, and even found followers in the non-Slavic regions of Italy and the south of France.

church—called the Bosnian Church—which the pope never officially recognized. Historians' opinions differ on how similar the Bosnian Church was to Catholicism. Some say it was more like Bogomilism, while others insist it was very close to traditional Catholicism.

It seems that Bosnia was constantly at war throughout the Middle Ages. However, not all the fighting was based on religion or ethnicity. Indeed, on many occasions royalty and other nobles intermarried. When it suited their strategic interests, rulers thought nothing of changing religions or forming political alliances with people of other faiths. When fighting was not about religion or ethnic pride, it was often about acquiring more territory to expand kingdoms. Other times it had more to do with getting rich, which was accomplished by plundering merchant caravans traveling inland and back from cities on the Adriatic.

The Ottoman Empire

About 1322, Ban Stephan Kotromanić (d. 1353) took over as ruler of Bosnia and began to make amends with Hungary. Thanks to his diplomacy, Bosnia and Hungary became close allies. Ban Stephan Kotromanić supported Hungary in its battles with neighboring Croatia so when parts of Croatia fell, Kotromanić was able to claim for himself some of the territory. When Serbia was involved in civil fighting following the death of its king in 1321, Kotromanić expanded his kingdom by gaining control of much of a Serbian district called Hum five years later.

This hand-tinted photograph depicts a medieval Ottoman Turk, most likely a soldier, such as those who conquered Bosnia. (Courtesy Free Library of Philadelphia)

Following Kotromanić's death in battle against Serbia in 1353, his nephew Ban Stephan Tvrtko I (1338–91) became ruler. Like his uncle, Tvrtko was a strong leader. By the 1370s he controlled the rest of Hum as well as additional territories to the north, and in 1377, in the Serbian town of Mileševo, he was crowned king of Serbia and Bosnia (the title "king" replaced "ban") Bosnia at that time was as big a nation as it would ever become. Its borders extended from the Sava River to the north to the islands of Korčula and Hvar in the south.

But Bosnia's domination was not to last. On June 28, 1389, Tvrtko and his fellow Bosnians were given a taste of what was to come. The armies of the Ottoman Turks, who had begun to build their huge empire, met the Serbian king Lazar (1329–89) in a district of Serbia called Kosovo. Fighting between the Muslim Turks and the Orthodox Christian Serbs broke out in Kosovo Polje, or "Plain of the Blackbirds." King Lazar was captured and killed, and the Serbs were defeated. Once proud Serbia was now under the control of the Ottoman Empire.

The Ottomans quickly made forays into Bosnia. Meanwhile, the leader of Hum, Stephan Vukcić (1404–66), was beginning to assert his own independence from Bosnia. His title, *vojvoda*, implied that he was ranked under the king of Bosnia, but in 1448, he took the title *herzeg* of Hum (and the Coast). *Herzeg* is derived from the German *Herzog*, meaning "duke." Thus his dominion became known as Herzegovina.

However, Vukcić's new title hardly mattered because the mighty Ottoman Empire continued making further incursions into his region. It captured the city of Vrhbosna in 1451. By 1465, the rest of Bosnia had fallen, and in 1481 Herzegovina had been conquered.

The rule of the Ottoman Turks was not the only event to bring change to Bosnia. In 1492, a major occurrence took place that had little to do with Christopher Columbus or the age of exploration. The entire Jewish population—some 70,000 people—were expelled from Spain.

Spain was not yet a unified country but a confederation of states, each with their own leaders. The Muslim Moors, originally from North Africa, had controlled parts of it since the 700s. In the 15th century, Spanish Catholics tried to regain control of the entire land, and, in 1492, Granada was the last Spanish kingdom still occupied by Muslims. Ferdinand of Aragon and Isabella of Castile became king and queen and immediately forced all Jews and many Muslims to leave. Many non-Catholics were brutally murdered. Those who could, fled, and a large number of Jews traveled east, settling in Vrhbosna.

The Ottoman Turks did not treat other religions as equals to Islam, but they were more tolerant than Spanish Christians. Non-Muslims could not vote nor own property and had to pay taxes Muslims were not required to pay. However, they were permitted to peacefully practice their own religion.

Many Bosnians converted to Islam. In fact, many more Bosnians than Croats or Serbs converted. Why remains a mystery, but historians have made some educated guesses. Some who converted, like the remaining Bogomils, were members of the ruling classes and did not wish to lose their land and privileges. Others recognized there were financial and other benefits to believing in the same religion as those who ruled them, such as the right to vote, to own property, and to pay lower taxes. Still others believed that God must have been on the side of the Muslims because God allowed Muslims to conquer the Christians.

But why did so many Bosnians—as opposed to other Slavs—convert? One theory is that Bosnians had a history of being at odds with the Christian Church, so converting was not a major jolt to their belief systems. Christians who converted to Islam were known as Bosniaks.

Other historians point out that some Christians became Muslims against their will. In a system known as *devsirme* (DEV-seer-me), young Christian males were regularly taken from their families, converted, and made servants to the Ottoman rulers. Those who did not become servants were drafted into the Ottoman army, where they became indoctrinated with Muslim beliefs.

Despite their involuntary conversions, some of these boys did very well. One of these was an Orthodox Christian named Mehmet Sokolović (after conversion he became known as Mehmet Sokollu) who was brought to Istanbul to attend school. He gradually worked his way up the ranks until as a grown man he was appointed to the position of grand vizier, second in power to the ruling sultan, the Ottoman equivalent of a king. Ultimately, most nobles became Muslims while the vast majority of peasants remained Christian.

The Ottomans divided the land into three units, called *sandzaks*. The *sandzaks* were Bosnia, Herzegovina, and Zvornik, which was composed of much of present-day Serbia, and all were governed by a *sandzak-beg* who was appointed by the sultan. The *sandzaks* were all part of a larger district, or *beglerbeglik*, called Rumeli, which was governed by a *beglerbeg*.

Bosnia grew rapidly in both size and importance and in the 1550s was designated as a *beglerbeglik*. Its capital, Vrhbosna, thrived and grew into a sparkling cultural, educational, and political center of the Ottoman Empire. Craftsmen, such as sword makers, leather workers, blacksmiths, millers, bakers, and saddlers opened businesses and thrived. These workers organized themselves, establishing some of the world's first guilds, the forerunners of today's labor unions.

Dozens of mosques (Islamic places of worship) and hundreds of public schools were built. An intricate infrastructure took shape. By the mid-1500s Vrhbosna had been fitted with wooden pipes that brought running water to private homes, mosques, and government buildings. Fountains decorated mosque courtyards, and Turkish baths attracted the work-weary who needed to rest and relax. Dozens of inns provided food and lodging for caravans traveling from places such as Istanbul, Venice, and Vienna.

About that time, Vrhbosna underwent a name change. The *sandzek-beg* referred to his home as a *saraj*, which is Turkish for "palace" or "castle." The ruling Ottomans then called the city Saraj-ovasi. *Ovas* means "field." In the Bosnian dialect, the name became *Sarajevo* (pronounced SA-RA-YAY-VOE).

As with many empires, in time cracks appeared in the foundation of the Ottoman Empire. First of all, a larger power controlled much of central Christian Europe to the north. The Hapsburg Empire of Austria, run by a German family, was continually at odds with the Ottomans on religious and other matters. The two empires fought from 1683 to 1697: The Hapsburgs won. As a result, an agreement called the Treaty of Karlowitz was signed in 1699, giving the Hapsburgs rule over much of central Europe, including most of Croatia, Hungary, and Slavonia. Some experts say this treaty "marked the beginning of the Ottoman Empire's disintegration."

Although the Ottomans had shown more tolerance than others toward different religions, Bosnian Christians began to feel they were neglected by their leaders. Many were lowly serfs who labored to build spacious manors for Turkish noblemen. In time, even Bosnian Muslims started to feel that the Ottoman rulers, located in faraway Istanbul, were ignoring their needs.

Ottoman control over Bosnia and Herzegovina declined through the 1700s. While the Turks and Hapsburgs were engaged in repeated struggles, Bosnians were often caught in the middle and, inevitably, the standard of living for the region's citizens deteriorated. By the 1800s, Bosnia and Herzegovina were backwaters compared to the rest of Europe. As the Industrial Revolution swept over most of Europe in the early 1800s it seemed to pass over this part of the continent. The majority of Bosnians were illiterate, and most of those still earned their living by tilling the land for the Muslim nobility. Machines speedily made textiles and other manufactured goods elsewhere in Europe, but here no one had machines. In Bosnia goods were made slowly by hand as they had been for hundred of years.

Rebellion

It was only natural, then, that, being left out of such a progressive revolution, the vast majority of Bosnians lived in poverty. Even their immediate neighbors thrived compared to the people of Bosnia and Herzegovina. The citizens of Croatia, under the rule of the Hapsburgs, used modern machinery in both factories and farms to increase production and bring in money. The people of Serbia, directly east of Bosnia, had revolted and expelled the Ottomans earlier in the 1800s and governed themselves. They had streamlined the ways of growing crops, which made them wealthier than the Bosnians. By the mid-1800s Bosnia was the last European outpost of the now weak Ottoman Empire. The people in Bosnia were ready for a change.

Poverty-stricken Christian peasants in Herzegovina rebelled against the Muslim nobles in 1875. They wanted better living conditions from their landlords. However, as Orthodox Christians they had much more in common with the Serbs than with Turkish Muslims. It was not long before their revolution called for unity with Serbia. This occurrence is known as both the Christian Rebellion and the Peasant Rebellion.

The Ottoman army responded by burning hundreds of peasant villages, causing poor Bosnian refugees to escape to Serbia, Croatia, and another republic, Montenegro, located to Bosnia's south, which had been quasi-independent since 1852. Serbia supported the rebels and, along with the republic of Montenegro, declared war on the Ottomans in 1876. Their goal was to annex Bosnia.

The Serbs were supported by another major power: Russia. Mighty Russia was not so different from other empires in that it wanted power in the Balkans. The Russians hoped to defeat the Ottomans, so they declared war against them in 1877.

Southeastern Europe was soon engulfed in all-out war. The Russians made quick gains against the Ottomans. The rest of Europe was suspicious of the Russians and concerned by its attempts at expansion. A meeting between the major European powers, known as the Berlin Congress, was called in Berlin, Germany, in June 1878. Its results would affect the lives of the people in the region for decades.

The Europeans and Ottomans came to an agreement that divided their influences in the Balkans. Much of the nation of Bulgaria, to the east, had been swallowed up by the Russian invaders and was returned to the Ottomans. Meanwhile, to maintain a balance of power, Bosnia and Herzegovina were to be governed by the Kingdom of Austria-Hungary, the core of the Hapsburg Empire. (Though today two separate nations, Austria and Hungary were then the center of the Hapsburg Empire.)

Austro-Hungarian Rule

Legally, Bosnia and Herzegovina were still part of the Ottoman Empire. But they were put under the "occupation and administration" of Austria-Hungary. The official term for Bosnia and Herzegovina's status was *corpus separatum*, which meant it was given freedom to govern itself and did not officially belong to Austria-Hungary. Four Austro-Hungarian imperial military divisions, totaling 72,000 soldiers, marched into Bosnia and Herzegovina on July 31, 1878. The European occupation of little Bosnia and Herzegovina had begun; for the first time in more than 400 years, the Bosnians were no longer under Muslim rule.

This did not sit well with the Bosnian Muslims. They immediately rebelled against their new occupiers but the Austro-Hungarians subdued them within a matter of months. In order to prevent more Muslim uprisings, the Austro-Hungarians made only a few changes in the agrarian system made up of Muslim landlords and Christian serfs. No radical changes meant that things would stay as they had for centuries.

However, industry did come to Bosnia: everything from steel mills to power plants. Bustling Sarajevo was the site of Bosnia's first tobacco

Sarajevo has always been the cultural center of Bosnia. This photo shows the Bosnian capital in the 1890s. (Courtesy Library of Congress)

factory in 1880, a carpet-making mill in 1888, and a soap plant in 1894. For the first time Bosnia had railway lines and secondary schools.

At this time, in 1882, Austria-Hungary's finance minister, Benjamin von Kállay, introduced the new concept of *bosnjastvo,* or "Bosnianism." The idea was for the people of Bosnia to identify as one nation, as opposed to more specific ethnic and religions identities such as Serbs, Croats, Catholics, Muslims, and Orthodox Christians. Kállay and the Bosnian rulers tried hard to make Bosnianism work, going so far as to build Sarajevo's Provincial Museum to celebrate Bosnians as a unified people.

Kállay hoped that Bosnianism would keep the ethnic and religious groups from fighting and discourage the growth of Croatian and Serbian nationalism in Bosnia. But the people living here never saw themselves as mere Bosnians. Their religious and ethnic identities were too entrenched for Kállay's idea to work.

The Austro-Hungarians recognized the failure of Bosnianism, and after Kállay died in 1903, István Burián (1851–1922), his replacement, steered clear of any such meddling. He allowed religious and ethnic groups to celebrate their individual identities and gave them limited independence. Some formed their own political parties and started their own publications.

In 1908, after 30 years of ruling Bosnia as if it were a legal part of its kingdom, Austria-Hungary abandoned the idea of *corpus separatum* and formally annexed Bosnia and Herzegovina. This removed any possibility that the Ottomans might legally reclaim the area and entitled Bosnians to the full rights of Austria-Hungary's other citizens, including complete freedom of religion. A Bosnian parliament was formally assembled.

At first, other European nations objected, as did some Bosnians. Austria-Hungary compensated the Ottomans in cash for their new subjects. In time, the Bosnians, the Ottomans, and the rest of Europe approved the annexation.

One group that did not approve was the Serbs. They maintained that the Orthodox Christians of Bosnia should be connected with Serbia, not with Austria-Hungary, which they considered the occupying kingdom. In addition, Serbia's leaders had their own desire to expand. In October 1912, with their allies Montenegro, Bulgaria, and Greece, they invaded the nation of Turkey. Formed out of the remnants of the Ottoman Empire, Turkey had lost its former power and surrendered much of its territory to the four Balkan invaders. This conflict has become known as the First Balkan War.

The war ended on May 30, 1913, with the signing of a treaty in London. In defeat, Turkey gave into the demands of the Balkan allies. A jelly bean-shaped stretch of land south of Montenegro and west of Serbia became the nation of Albania. Serbia and Montenegro nearly doubled in size. War broke out again in the Balkans just a month later, and on August 10 another peace treaty was signed.

The Black Hand

Yet the end of the Balkan Wars was only the proverbial calm before the storm. A secret society in Serbia known as the Black Hand was brewing trouble that would eventually affect not just Serbia but all of Europe.

Gavrilo Princip was a teenager when he assassinated Archduke Francis Ferdinand, starting the chain reaction of events leading to the onset of World War I. (Courtesy Free Library of Philadelphia)

The Black Hand was a group of radical Serbians who believed that Bosnia and Herzegovina should be part of Serbia, not Austria-Hungary. It was headed by a man named Dragutin Dimitrijević, an officer in the Serbian army.

Mass confusion reigns as assassin Gavrilo Princip is captured in Sarajevo in 1914. (Courtesy Free Library of Philadelphia)

One rank-and-file member was a 19-year-old postman's son named Gavrilo (or "Gabriel") Princip (1894–1918). When Dimitrijević learned that the heir to the throne of Austria-Hungary, Archduke Francis Ferdinand, planned to visit Sarajevo on June 28, 1914, he dispatched Princip and seven other Black Hand members on a sinister mission: to assassinate the archduke.

On June 28, Francis Ferdinand and his wife, Sophie, traveled down Appel Quay, one of Sarajevo's main streets, in the second car of a six-car motorcade. The eight assassins were scattered along the avenue. As assembled crowds cheered, Nedjelko Čabrinović, one of Princip's fellow would-be assassins, tossed a bomb at the archduke injuring many but missing its main target. Later, on the way to the hospital, the archduke's driver happened to stop in front of a food store that Gavrilo Princip was leaving. Seeing the archduke five feet in front of him, Princip realized that Čabrinović's bombing attempt had failed. Princip pulled a pistol from his pocket and fired two shots. He hit both the archduke and his wife, and they died shortly afterward. Few could have realized at that moment that a teenager with a gun had just started World War I.

NOTES

p. 6 "'golden age of Kulin Ban.'" Thierry Domin, "History of Bosnia and Herzegovina from the Origins to 1992," North Atlantic Treaty Organisation. Available on-line. URL: http://www.nato.int/sfor/indexinf/122/p03a/chapter2.htm. Downloaded August 29, 2002.

p. 11 "'marked the beginning . . .'" *The Columbia Encyclopedia*, 6th ed. "Karlowitz, Treaty of," Bartleby.com. Available on-line. URL: http://www.bartleby.com/65/ka/Karlowit.html. Downloaded August 30, 2002.

p. 13 "Four Austro-Hungarian imperial . . ." Robert J. Donia and John V. A. Fine, Jr., *Bosnia and Herzegovina: A Tradition Betrayed* (New York: Columbia University Press, 1994), p. 93.

2

FROM WORLD WAR I
THROUGH TITO

The situation in Europe in 1914 was a firecracker waiting for someone to light the fuse. Gavrilo Princip did just that when he pulled the trigger and murdered Archduke Francis Ferdinand, and his wife, Sophie.

The war did not start immediately. Austria-Hungary gave Serbia a 10-point ultimatum and 48 hours to respond. The Serbs agreed right away to most points, but refused one: allowing Austria-Hungary to take an active part on Serbian land to investigate the murders. As a result, the two nations broke off diplomatic relations on July 25, 1914. Just three days later, Austria-Hungary declared war on Serbia.

Right away, the nations of Europe took sides. Russia announced it would support Serbia. Germany said it would side with Austria-Hungary. Regarding the assassination, the Austro-Hungarian emperor, Francis Joseph, said to Germany's ruler, Kaiser Wilhelm I, "Their [Serbia's] policy of uniting all southern Slavs under the Serbian flag encourages such crimes. Serbia must be eliminated as a political factor in the Balkans."

The kaiser had been eager to expand his territory and the start of war was a perfect opportunity to do so. On August 2, Germany invaded Luxembourg; on August 3 it declared war against France and Russia; on August 4 it invaded Belgium, motivating Britain to enter the war to protect Belgium.

The United States declared neutrality on August 5 and the next day Austria-Hungary declared war on Russia. Immediately Serbia declared war on Germany.

Within a few short weeks, war had broken out all over the European continent. Germany, Austria-Hungary, and its allies were known collectively as the Central Powers, while Britain, France, Russia, and their supporters became the Entente Powers.

Even though the war started in Sarajevo, very little fighting happened in Bosnia. As Hapsburg subjects, Bosnian men were drafted into the Austro-Hungarian military, but routinely deserted to join the Serbian army.

Of all the southern Slavs, the Serbs suffered the most at the hands of Austria-Hungary. As rebels against Austro-Hungarian leadership, Bosnian and Herzegovinan Serbs living near the border of Serbia were often sent to internment camps where they were abused. Others were deported. Some were put on trial for treason or for giving aid and comfort to the enemy. Those who were convicted were usually sentenced to long prison terms or capital punishment. By late 1915, Austria-Hungary overran Serbia and was firmly in control of the smaller country.

On April 6, 1917, the United States reconsidered its neutral position and joined the European war on the side of the Entente Powers. The tide began to turn against the Central Powers.

The Corfu Declaration

In July 1917, representatives of the independent nations of Serbia, Croatia, Montenegro, and Slovenia (a fairly small southern Slavic land north of Croatia) met on Corfu, one of the Greek islands, to consider what would become of their peoples when the fighting ended. There were two principal negotiators. One was an exiled Croatian leader named Ante Trumbić (1864–1938). The other was Serbian prime minister Nikola Pašić (1845–1926).

Pašić, speaking for Serbia, was hoping to expand his homeland with territory from Austria-Hungary, after the empire's anticipated defeat. Trumbić, on the other hand, wanted to unify the southern Slavs. He talked of a union of Croats, Slovenes, and Serbs. As Russia, Serbia's biggest supporter was at the time distracted by the Russian Revolution,

Pašić knew he could not count on them for help and so he gave in. On July 27, 1917, Trumbić and his supporters announced what became known as the Corfu Declaration. They declared that there would be a new nation made up of the southern Slavic republics.

This new nation would have a constitution and an elected parliament, but would be ruled by a king. Each people's flag would be recognized. Each of their languages and alphabets would be recognized, as would each of their religions.

By the fall of 1918, Austria-Hungary's emperor Charles I knew he was being defeated. The Austrian people had become tired living under the iron thumb of an emperor, and Austrian students and workers took to the streets in protest, calling out en masse, "Down with the Hapsburgs!" Charles I had no choice but to resign and declare Austria-Hungary a republic. In October the emperor was forced to leave Vienna, the capital. On November 11, 1918, Germany surrendered and World War I was over.

A New Kingdom

Then, on December 1, Serbian crown prince Alexander Obrenović announced the official formation of a new nation: the Kingdom of Serbs, Croats, and Slovenes. He would be known as King Alexander. The kingdom's capital would be the Serbian city of Belgrade.

Bosnia and Herzegovina joined the new kingdom. Bosnian Christians, tired of living in an agrarian society under Muslim landlords, wanted total reform. Bosnia's Muslims were generally supportive of a South Slav state, but supported as little agrarian reform as possible.

Christian peasants, especially Serbs, withheld payments to Muslim landlords. Indeed, many physically attacked Muslims. The unrest did not cease until Bosnia's provincial government asked Serbian troops to enter Bosnia to help stop the violence. Still, the disorder was not halted right away.

So now the people had a pan-Slavic kingdom. Was this the dream come true for the southern Slavs?

They certainly tried to make it so. Political parties representing the many factions were formed. Bosnian Muslims formed the Yugoslav ("South Slav") Muslim Organization (YMO), led by Mehmed Spaho (1883–1939). Bosnian Croats championed the Croatian Peasant Party, under the leadership of Stjepan Radić (1871–1928), and the Communist Party of Yugoslavia (CPY) tried to organize industrial laborers and down-trodden agricultural workers.

Bosnian Serbs split their loyalties between two parties. The Serbian Radical Party under the leadership of the former prime minister, Nikola Pašić (1845–1926), was the stronger of the two and it favored strong Serbian influence in the kingdom. The Serbian Democratic Party advocated a more moderate approach to Serb leadership.

However, it was not long before the new kingdom began to crumble from within. On June 28, 1921, the anniversary of the 14th-century battle of Kosovo Polje, in which the Ottoman Empire had defeated Serbia, the national assembly met to vote on a constitution. A Serbian king already headed the nation but the Serbian Radical Party insisted on gaining more power. They said they would recognize Bosnia and Herzegovina's original borders only as part of a constitution that adopted a centralized Serbian leadership in the kingdom.

The YMO overwhelmingly voted for the new constitution, while some, like the Croats and Communists, thought the constitution was so unfair that they boycotted the meeting. With more radical Serbs and members of the YMO in attendance than other party members, the constitution passed. It was named the Vidovdan Constitution since it was passed on St. Vitus's Day, a Christian holiday honoring the martyred third century saint ("Vidovdan" is a local name for the day).

The Communist Party got themselves in trouble almost immediately. Members tried—but failed—to assassinate King Alexander shortly after the nation's constitution was approved. Then they succeeded in assassinating the kingdom's interior minister. In response, the Skupština, the kingdom's national assembly, passed a law banning the existence of the Communist Party of Yugoslavia.

That was not the only immediate difficulty. The Croatian Peasant Party continued to boycott the federal assembly until a group of Muslims and others excluded from the assembly overthrew the Serbian Radical Party, which controlled the assembly. For the next several years the parties jockeyed for leadership. No party ever had complete control.

Because Mehmet Spaho was such a skilled leader, he was able to give the Muslims of Bosnia and Herzegovina a steady voice in the kingdom. Locally, the Bosnian Muslims attempted to reform the agricultural system

Even in the early 20th century, Bosnian agriculture was based on a system of serfs and landlords. Here, Christian peasants thresh grain in the Bosnian countryside sometime between 1890 and 1900. (Courtesy Library of Congress)

in their district where Christian peasants continued to work the land as serfs for Muslim owners as they had for centuries. In the 20th century, that system was wholly out of date and patently unfair to the workers.

For most of the 1920s, the kingdom's lawmakers worked to better the lives of Christian serfs and to find fair ways to compensate long-time landowners. First, serfdom was outlawed. Huge Muslim-owned properties were divided into sections, and most peasants were allowed to own land they had cultivated. The government paid the landlords cash and bonds in exchange for their land.

The solution should have satisfied everybody, but some historians say it satisfied no one. For the most part, the lands the Christian serfs had cultivated were relatively small, which meant they had to make a living from fairly unsuitable plots. Many of the Muslim landowners, meanwhile, felt their compensation did not equal the value of the land they had given up.

A Heated Argument Turns Violent

All the while in the rest of the kingdom, the old ethnic and religious rivalries between the varied southern Slavic peoples continued. By the late 1920s these had risen to serious levels. Chief among the arguing parties were the Serbs and the Croats. Stjepan Radić, head of the Croatian Peasant Party, believed his people were not allowed the power they deserved while living under King Alexander and the Serbian-controlled legislature. Radić constantly resorted to boycotts and other forms of disrupting legislative sessions. He continued as the Croatian leader until June 20, 1928, when tragedy struck the parliament of the Kingdom of the Serbs, Croats, and Slovenes.

During a particularly ferocious debate, Radić and four other Croatians were shot and killed by a Radical Party delegate from Montenegro. The Croatian members of parliament stormed out. Charges and counter-charges followed, and protesters on all sides took to the streets. Complete disorder in the kingdom was the rule for the next six months. Radić's successor, Vlatko Maček (1879–1964), was put on trial for terrorism and was sent to prison.

Finally, on January 6, 1929, King Alexander took control of the situation by declaring the kingdom's constitution invalid. He abolished the legislature, cancelled local self-government, did away with most civil liberties, and declared himself the absolute ruler of the Kingdom of the Serbs, Croats, and Slovenes. He also gave his realm a new name: the Kingdom of Yugoslavia, or Kingdom of the South Slavs.

Hoping to stem ethnic and religious strife, Alexander tried an unusual tactic: He got rid of the traditional provinces, including Bosnia and Herzegovina, Serbia, and Croatia. He redrew the map of the kingdom and replaced the old provinces with nine new ones called *banovinas*. The leader of each *banovina* was a *ban*, the same title used by regional rulers 700 years earlier. Most *banovinas* were named for rivers flowing through them. Bosnia and Herzegovina's former land was included in four of the *banovinas*. These were named Drina, Primorska, Vrbas, and Zeta.

But the distribution of the *banovinas* was not fair. It favored the Serbs who constituted a majority of the population in six of them. Leaders of the YMO, including Mehmet Spaho, though not happy with the new alignment of their country, reluctantly gave it their approval.

That was not so unusual. Many ordinary Yugoslavs at first supported the dictatorship thinking that without so many parties vying for control, the new system would reduce corruption and streamline the government.

But even without a parliamentary system, Yugoslavia's ethnic groups continued to fight for either honest representation in government or more control over others. The only difference was this time they took their disagreements to the streets. Public protests were often broken up by police and were often violent.

In 1931, Alexander eased up on his absolute power. On September 3, he announced the kingdom would once more have a constitution under which political parties would be legal. The king would still be able to hire and fire government officials and ethnic- or religion-based organizations would continue to be banned.

At this time, everyday life was not going well in Yugoslavia—or in most of the world. The Great Depression, which began in the United States in 1929, had spread throughout the world. Southeastern Europe was no exception. Because there were no markets for their products, everyone from miners to farmers was out of work. The farms in Bosnia, whose economy was still mainly based on agriculture, lay in ruins. Those that were worked produced small yields.

Yugoslavia Under the Regency Council

Troubles for Yugoslavia continued in October 1934 when King Alexander was assassinated while visiting Marseilles, France. The assassin, Petrus Kalemen, was a member of an ultra-nationalist Croatian group called Ustaša (Ustasha), which translates as "insurrectionists." The Ustaša allied with the newly fascist states of Italy, under Benito Mussolini (1883–1945), and Germany, ruled by Adolf Hitler (1889–1945). Their goal was to end the Yugoslavian kingdom and establish a separate nation of Croatia.

Alexander had written in his will that his son Peter should be king upon his own death. However, when Alexander died Peter was just 11 years old. So a regency council consisting of three men led by Alexander's cousin Prince Pavle (1893–1976) was chosen to lead the Yugoslav government until Peter came of age.

Just a few months after taking office, Pavle and the other regents allowed Yugoslavia to take a few more steps toward democracy. First, his government allowed Vlatko Maček to be freed from prison, which pleased the Croats. Then in June 1935 he named a Serb, Milan Stojadinović (1888–1961), to the office of prime minister. In an effort to please the

Bosnian Muslims, Stojadinović named Mehmet Spaho his minister of transportation.

Stojadinović remained in power until 1939 when he began to lose popularity. While he had edged his country closer to democracy, he had also developed friendly trade relations with Mussolini's Italy and Hitler's Germany. Prince Pavle replaced him in February 1939 with a new prime minister named Dragiša Cvetković (1893–1969). Mehmet Spaho and the Bosnian Muslims gave their support, as usual, to the new government.

But like Stojadinović, Cvetković leaned toward an alliance with Nazi Germany because Germany had made strong investments in Yugoslavian industry. Like much of the world, Yugoslavia was mired in the tough times of the Great Depression. However, in a four-month period starting in November 1940, Germany occupied or coerced concessions from Yugoslavia's neighbors Hungary, Bulgaria, and Romania. Yugoslavs were concerned that they were next.

The Cvetković government lasted longer than the previous one, but on March 27, 1941, members of the Yugoslav military overthrew Cvetković and named as king Alexander's son Peter II. Peter was just 17 years old. That night the people of Belgrade celebrated, since they were certain the new king would be no friend of Hitler. Nearly all the factions in Yugoslavia, including most Bosnian Muslims and Croats, supported the government. But Germany's Adolf Hitler was irate.

War, Again

Just 10 days later, on April 6, the teenage king was stunned by the sounds of bombs being dropped over Belgrade. The German Luftwaffe, or air force, was attacking Yugoslavia in an attempt to rid Yugoslavia of their unfriendly king and expand the fascist German empire. Germany never even announced a formal declaration of war.

The Luftwaffe continued bombing Belgrade, killing approximately 20,000 people in just three days. Then the Germans began a ground invasion, attacking Yugoslavia from territory in recently captured Romania and Bulgaria. Meanwhile, Germany's ally Italy attacked eastern regions of the kingdom. King Peter and his staff were evacuated to London and on April 17, Yugoslavia unconditionally surrendered to Germany.

In the early spring of 1941, Germany invaded Bosnia and Herzegovina. In this photograph, German troops raise the Nazi flag at Sarajevo City Hall on April 16 that year. (AP/Wide World Photos)

The period of World War II in Yugoslavia, 1941–45, was filled with carnage, heroism, and intrigue. The Nazis created a new district in the center of Yugoslavia called the Independent State of Croatia, consisting of both Croatia and Bosnia and Herzegovina. But there was nothing independent about it. The Nazis put in charge a puppet leader named Ante Pavelić (1889–1959). Pavelić was the head of the fascist Ustaša, and historians believe he was behind the assassination of King Alexander seven years earlier. Pavelić ruled his newly organized state with instructions from Hitler.

Their enemies were the Jews, Serbs, and Roma (Gypsies) living there. Some Serbs were either forced to convert to Catholicism or were put to death. Others were simply murdered. There was no options for Jews and Roma. Their property was confiscated and they were sent to death camps.

Interestingly, Bosnian Muslims were spared such genocide. The Ustaša regarded them as Croatian Catholics who had merely rejected their native religion. Since the Ustaša believed they were Catholics by nature, they were not forced to convert as the Serbs were. In fact, many Muslims, including YMO activists, collaborated with the Ustaša's killings. In parts of what had been Bosnia and Herzegovina-Serbia, they deliberately attacked and murdered Serbs.

In response to the Nazi-approved Ustaša brutality, resistance forces were born. One group was the Serbian Četniks (Chetniks), who took their name from Serbians who fought against the Ottomans several decades earlier. They saw themselves as the official representatives of King Peter II's government in exile. They thought nothing of avenging their countrymen with brutality of their own.

The other group was the Partisans, led by a man named Josip Broz (1892–1980). The Partisans were communists and although the Communist Party had been outlawed, Broz was a skilled leader and managed in the late 1930s to help organize a Yugoslav branch of what was seen as a pariah party. Broz was also known by a code name he chose for himself: Tito. Tito and the Partisans' motto was "Death to Fascism; Freedom to the People." That, along with a charismatic personality, helped Tito win followers.

But the campaigns against the mighty German military would not be easy. In late 1941, the Četniks who abhorred the idea of communism,

The medieval city of Jajce is best known for its historic houses with angled roofs. But it played a role in another historic era when in 1943 Tito and his anti-fascists met there to make postwar plans. (Courtesy Free Library of Philadelphia)

turned against the Partisans, attacking them and supporting Germany and Italy. They felt that a fascist victory would be better than a communist one.

By the fall of 1942, the Partisans, as the only real organized Yugoslav enemy of the fascists, had the support of many noncommunists. But the Partisans were in a way fighting two wars: one against the fascist invaders and another against their fellow Yugoslavs, the Četniks. In November 1942, the Partisans met in the town of Bihać in northwest Bosnia. The group called itself the Antifascist Council for the National Liberation of Yugoslavia (in Serbo-Croatian its acronym is known as AVNOJ). They announced they would support democracy, equal rights for all ethnic groups, and a free enterprise economic system.

Over the course of the next year, Italy surrendered and the Partisans took control of sections of Yugoslavia that Italy had controlled. Tito called a second AVNOJ meeting in November 1943 in a medieval Bosnian capital city, Jajce. There they began making plans for leading Yugoslavia after the war was over. Tito would be the marshal and prime minister of Yugoslavia and King Peter would not be welcomed back until a vote had been taken on what should be done with the monarchy. A month later, the leaders of the big three allies—Franklin Roosevelt of the United States, Joseph Stalin of the Soviet Union, and Winston Churchill of Great Britain—met in a famous conference in Tehran, Iran. Early in the war they had supported the Četniks, but following the Tehran meeting, they formally announced they were throwing their full support behind the Partisans.

The Partisans enjoyed some of their strongest support from Bosnians. Since much of the brutal Ustaša consisted of both Bosnian Croats and Bosnian Muslims, they were afraid of being singled out for retaliation. But the Partisans set rules for their fighters in response to those concerns. For example, if Bosnian Muslims and Croats were forced to leave their homes to join in the resistance elsewhere, Partisans would guard their houses so they would not be damaged by vengeance-seeking Partisan Serbs. Such promises were not always easy to keep in wartime, but they were kept often enough to keep Bosnians on their side.

The Partisans and the Allies, particularly the Soviet Union's Red Army, battled and gradually wore down the Nazis in Yugoslavia. After liberating Belgrade late in 1944, they pressed on, finally liberating Sarajevo on April 6, 1945. On May 15, the Germans and Ustaša gave up, surrendering to the Partisans.

Titoism

Tito was going to run Yugoslavia according to his political ideal as a communist nation. However, one must keep in mind that there are different forms of communism. The Soviet Union—the other major world power along with the United States—was a communist country. The Soviets had fought with the Allies to liberate Europe from German and Italian fascism, and as a result Soviet troops occupied all the eastern European countries at the end of the war. Although Soviet premier Joseph Stalin promised these countries free and fair elections, that never happened. The Soviets ran them as communist dictatorships.

According to the original idea of communism, all businesses would be owned by the community, or the citizens of that particular country. There would be no private business. In the Soviet Union and in communist-controlled Eastern Europe, all businesses were owned by the government. The only official political party was the Communist Party. There was little tolerance for people with differing views. Citizens who openly criticized their government were usually punished. Religious worship was discouraged and, in some cases, outlawed.

Tito distanced himself from the Soviets' strong-armed leader Stalin and insisted on the independence of Yugoslavia. He developed a liberalized form of communism that became known across the world as Titoism.

Yugoslavia under Tito was a benign dictatorship. For example, he held elections in November 1945 for the national assembly, but there was only one slate of candidates, who were all Communists. Tito made an effort to industrialize and rebuild Yugoslavia following the war: The factories were owned not by private companies but by the federal government. Tito's Communist Party of Yugoslavia (CPY) broke up huge farms owned by single property owners. No single owner could possess more than 35 hectares (about 86.5 acres) of land. As a result, many Muslim landowners moved from the country to the cities.

However, there was no collective ownership of land under Tito, as there was in other communist European countries. Individuals owned the

President Tito and his wife, Jovanka, left, meet with U.S. president Richard Nixon and First Lady Pat Nixon (right) on October 28, 1971. (National Archives and Records Administration)

land they worked. While factories in the Soviet Union, and other communist European nations, were controlled from a distance by government officials, Tito allowed the laborers at Yugoslavian plants to form workers' councils. The councils were allowed to hire managers they wanted to work with, and to have a say in company policies. This style of running a business became known as socialist self-management.

The new Yugoslavian constitution, proclaimed on January 31, 1946, officially recognized five nationalities within its borders: the Slovenes, the Croats, the Serbs, the Macedonians, and the Montenegrins. At first, as they had been before in other governments, Bosnian Muslims were viewed as a separate class of people with no national identity. For years they claimed they were a nationality as well as a religious group. Finally, in 1968—22 years later—Bosnian Muslims were formally recognized by the official communist party, the League of Communists of Yugoslavia (LCY), as a sixth nationality.

The six traditional Yugoslav republics were also established: Slovenia, Croatia, Bosnia and Herzegovina, Serbia, Montenegro, and Macedonia.

JOSIP BROZ (MARSHAL TITO)

Under the leadership of Josip Broz, Marshal Tito, the people of Yugoslavia lived with a stability they had not seen for ages. His strong style of leadership, his ability to charm others, and his desire for independence made him a beloved and respected figure in his native land and throughout much of the world.

Josip Broz, one of 15 children, was born May 7, 1892, in the Croatian village of Kumrovec, near the border with Slovenia. His father, a blacksmith, was Croatian, and his mother was of Slovenian descent. In World War I, he fought on the side of Austria-Hungary against Russia. He was captured by the Russians but escaped and traveled to Petrograd, now St. Petersburg, where he took part in the Russian Revolution, siding with the Bolsheviks, or early Communists, against the leadership of Czar Nicholas II.

Broz returned home in 1920 where he found work as a metalworker. Impressed by communist ideals, Broz became an active union organizer before joining the Yugoslav Communist Party. Since membership in the Communist Party was officially against the law in the Kingdom of the Serbs, Croats, and Slovenes, Broz was arrested on the charge of organizing an illegal political party and sentenced to five years in prison. Some time after he was released from prison in 1934 he adopted the code name "Tito," and it soon became his official last name.

Tito's skill and bravery during World War II made him a national hero. As Yugoslavia's leader, his unique ideology won him many friends and some enemies. When he died on May 4, 1980, Yugoslavs showed an outpouring of grief. The fact that 49 world leaders attended his funeral proves that even in his later years he was a major player on the international stage.

Two districts of Serbia were declared autonomous, or under restricted self-rule: Vojvodina to the north and Kosovo to the southwest. Bosnia and Herzegovina was again an anomaly. With a population split between Serbian Orthodox Christians, Croatian Catholics, and Muslims, it was the only republic with no national majority. The six republics had little political power. For example, according to the new constitution, the republics had the right to secede from the federal union. However, it was

AMITY HIGH SCHOOL LIBRARY
WOODBRIDGE, CT 06525
36008392

considered that each had rejected that right when they opted to become part of the nation of Yugoslavia.

For much of the first three decades after the end of World War II, Bosnia blossomed like a rose. Because of ample supplies of water and minerals, the republic was well suited for industry, and since Bosnia is mountainous, and located at the center of Yugoslavia, it seemed a safe place for the defense industry and a good home to most of the nation's weapons manufactories. Industry had its down side: Clouds of smog blanketed Bosnia, especially Sarajevo. And with more and more workers trading rural lives for urban ones near the factories, areas suffered overcrowding. Many high-rise apartments had to be built to house the new arrivals.

When Croatians rebelled in the streets in the early 1970s, claiming they were taxed unfairly compared to the other republics, Tito cracked down on the protesters, arresting hundreds. Over the next year, Tito removed reformist party leaders in Macedonia, Serbia, Slovenia, and Vojvodina and replaced them with antireform politicians. To prevent further dissidence, Tito's supporters in the assembly met in 1974 and elected him president for life.

Yugoslav women pass in front of a power relay station in 1955, part of a project started by the Tito government to develop his country's natural resources for the purpose of trade with neighboring countries. (Courtesy of United Nations)

Of all the Yugoslav republics, Bosnia supported Tito the most. After all, Tito had deep roots there; his World War II–era Partisans emerged out of Bosnia. It was in the Bosnian cities of Bihać and Jajce that they met to discuss how to first fight the Nazis, then how to govern the nation after the war. His strongest party regulars remained in Bosnia.

By this time much of Yugoslavia's economy was beginning to be strained. This was due mostly to a huge amount of foreign debt and weakened industry. Some critics have said that Tito, by then in his early 80s, did little to correct his nation's financial woes.

NOTES

p. 18 "'Their [Serbia's] policy of uniting . . .'" *The Great War,* episode 1 (KCET/BBC Co-production, Community Television of Southern California, Executive Producer Blaine Baggett, 1996).

p. 25 "The Luftwaffe continued bombing . . ." Robert J. Donia and John V. A. Fine, Jr., *Bosnia and Herzegovina: A Tradition Betrayed* (New York: Columbia University Press, 1994), p. 134.

p. 27 "'Death to Fascism . . .'" Glenn E. Curtis, ed., *Yugoslavia: A Country Study* (Washington, D.C.: Library of Congress, 1992), p. 40.

3

YUGOSLAVIA'S DISINTEGRATION AND CIVIL WAR

In the late 1970s, Tito devised a system of government to take effect after his death. Instead of having a president for life, Yugoslavia would have a program of rotating presidents. Such an unusual form of government would have been unacceptable for almost any nation. However, in Yugoslavia, with its vibrant mixture of strong-willed ethnic and religious groups, there were hopes that such a system might actually work.

Tito had felt that in the absence of a strong, unifying leader, this method of governing would be the only one to hold the nation together, since no ethnic or religious group would be able to realistically claim that the government was ignoring them. A total of eight members of the presidency were chosen. These included representatives of each of the six republics and the two autonomous provinces, Vojvodina and Kosovo. Each would take turns as leader of the council for one year.

In theory, it might have worked. But there were two kinks in the plan. One was the fact that there would still be only one official party: the Communist Party. The other was the economy, which was continuing to sour.

In order to keep the economy from worsening to the point where it would be unmanageable, in 1981 the government ordered a study of their system. It was officially called the Long-Term Economic Stabilization Program. Unofficially, it was called the Krajgher Commission Report.

In 1983, after two years of debate and study, the report was released. Its main conclusion was that the current communist system of government-managed businesses, even with Tito's reforms, was not working. A free market economy had to be developed to some degree in order to spur growth. At the same time, the government passed what were called austerity measures. These included reducing government spending as a means of controlling inflation.

But getting the government officers to go along with the idea such of a free market economy was a major effort. If such a system was put into effect, the leaders of government bureaus in charge of economic affairs would lose much of their clout. Obviously, they did not want that. Nor did leaders of the Communist Party wish to give up their power to make government policies. So, little was done to attempt to bring the goals of the Krajgher Report to fruition.

The World Comes to Sarajevo

Amid all this stagnation, there was one bright spot in Yugoslavia—specifically Bosnia—in the early 1980s. The International Olympic Committee had selected Sarajevo as the site for the 1984 Winter Olympics. It was the first time, and to date the only time, any Olympic Games were held in the Balkans.

Much had to be done to prepare to host the world's greatest athletes in the Bosnian capital. The federal government gave the republic of Bosnia-Herzegovina ample funds to build lodging and athletic facilities. The city was spruced up: Dull, conformist buildings constructed under communist rule were repainted to look bright and new.

The Olympics turned out to be a huge success. A total of 49 nations with 1,278 athletes came to the mountains of Bosnia to compete for gold, silver, and bronze medals. Figure skater Katarina Witt of East Germany, and ice dancers Jayne Torville and Christopher Dean of Great Britain, became household names after stellar, winning performances. American brothers Phil and Steve Mahre earned gold and silver medals, respectively, in the men's Alpine slalom.

The world came to Sarajevo for the highly successful Winter Olympics of 1984. It is the only Olympics to be held in the Balkans. This shows the opening ceremonies on February 8, 1984. (AP/Wide World Photos)

Thanks to television coverage across the world, millions of people saw the beauty of the ancient city of Sarajevo and the lofty mountains surrounding it. More importantly to residents, the Olympics brought in millions of dollars to their financially strapped region.

The Agrokomerc Scandal

But once the good times of the Olympics were over, Bosnia and Yugoslavia returned to a huge economic mess. Industries stagnated and bureaucrats, concerned about their jobs, continued to block efforts toward reform. Reform was needed badly as was proven when a major scandal broke in 1987.

It all started with a fire. Early in the winter of 1987 flames destroyed a warehouse at a Bosnian company called Agrokomerc, located in a town called Velika Kladuša in the northwest section of the republic. Agrokomerc was thought by most to be one of the few success stories of Yugoslavian businesses that began under Tito.

However, while looking into damage caused by the fire, investigators from the Bosnian Ministry of Internal Affairs discovered that the financial foundation of Agrokomerc was built on unsecured loans of more than

$800 million. In other words, Agrokomerc did not have the actual money it needed to pay its employees and otherwise keep the business in operation. A total of 63 banks were involved in this ugly situation. One, the Bank of Bihać, closed right away and as a result, thousands of Agrokomerc workers were unable to cash their paychecks.

The scandal at Agrokomerc, as huge as it was, turned out to be just the beginning. It soon became apparent that the Bosnian member of the presidential council, Hamdija Požderac, was responsible for much of the bad debt at Agrokomerc. Požderac had been scheduled to become president of Yugoslavia the next year, but due to his involvement in the Agrokomerc scandal he was let go from the council on September 12, 1987.

Further investigations proved that Požderac was not the only Yugoslavian Communist Party official involved in the financial shenanigans at Agrokomerc. Roughly 200 party members from both Bosnia and Croatia were also let go from their positions.

One principal figure in the scandal, a Bosnian Muslim named Fikret Abdić, testified publicly that Agrokomerc was not an isolated case. According to Abdić, shady dealings like this were commonplace throughout the Yugoslavian business world.

It became clear that the system of self-management for which Tito had had such high hopes was not working. Corruption had ruined it. Powerful politicians, businessmen, and banks worked together to keep the Communist Party in control of Yugoslavian businesses. Instead of cooperating with workers' councils, many company managers took orders from Communist Party officials and more powerful managers. In return, they were given rewards of money. In addition, business leaders commonly bribed politicians to ignore dishonest practices at their companies.

The End of Communism

Workers became discouraged and angered by such widespread corruption. In the late 1980s, employees of many companies in Yugoslavia acted on this frustration by going on strike, something which they had hardly ever done during the first few decades of Tito's leadership. But in 1989 alone, a total of 1,900 strikes took place.

Unrest was not happening only in Yugoslavia. Throughout the Communist-run satellite nations of Eastern Europe, citizens who had had enough protested the corruption, their lack of freedom, and an economic system that did not work.

Then on November 9, 1989, the seemingly impossible happened. Communist East Germany opened the Berlin Wall. The wall had built in 1961 to keep East Germans from fleeing into free West Germany. Anticommunist demonstrators and massive crowds of freedom-hungry East Germans attacked the wall with hammers and other tools and literally tore it to pieces. They danced, sang, and cheered as the wall was destroyed.

The day after the Berlin Wall fell, the Communist leader of Bulgaria resigned. And as the decade of the 1980s was winding down, one communist government after another was overthrown or resigned under pressure as the people of these nations took to the streets in protest. Observers from across the globe were truly amazed at how fast so much change happened. After more than 40 years, it took mere weeks for the Communist bloc of Eastern Europe to crumble.

Yugoslavia Disintegrates

As in the past, Yugoslavia handled things differently from the other communist nations of Eastern Europe. There were no huge demonstrations to quicken the demise of communism. Instead, the old system died a slow, lingering death.

Much of its demise began with the actions of the president of Serbia, Slobodan Milošević (b. 1941), who had seized control of the office in 1989. In March that year, Milošević spearheaded a change in Serbia's constitution allowing the republic to annex what had been the autonomous districts of Vojdovina and Kosovo. They were then fully under Serbian control and their own governments were eliminated. By making such a bold move, Milošević gave the communist federal leadership a slap in the face.

Yugoslavia's central Communist Party barely made it into the new decade. Between Milošević strong-arming Vojdovina and Kosovo into submission, the economy continuing in a tailspin, and communist governments collapsing throughout Eastern Europe, Yugoslavia's federal

Slobodan Milošević, president of rump Yugoslavia, waves to workers at a car and weapons factory in 2000. Milošević has been accused of ethnic cleansing. (AP/Wide World Photos)

leadership faced enormous difficulties. At a meeting in January 1990 the party attempted in a last-ditch effort to save their nation. However, when the leaders of Slovenia demanded more regional power, and when the Communist Party refused to give it, the Slovenians walked out of the conference.

Without Slovenia, the communist federal government's dream of a united Yugoslavia was ruined. In the early hours of the morning of January 23, 1990, the League of Communists of Yugoslavia officially ended the conference, never to regroup again.

Over the course of 1990, each republic held its own elections. In Bosnia and Herzegovina, the three biggest parties were comprised mostly of citizens of each of Bosnia's three main ethnic groups.

This is not to say that every aspect of the average Bosnian citizens' lives was ruled by their ethnicity. While most Bosnians were proud of their personal backgrounds, they freely intermingled with each other. People of all ethnic groups lived together in the numerous high-rise apartments that had been built in Bosnian urban neighborhoods under Tito. They also worked and went to school together, and frequently intermarried. By 1990, roughly 40 percent of urban Bosnian marriages were mixed.

In November, Bosnia and Herzegovina held their elections. A noncommunist named Alija Izetbegović (b. 1925) of the Muslim-dominated Party of Democratic Action (SDA) became president. The SDA won a

ALIJA IZETBEGOVIĆ

To Bosnian Muslims, Alija Izetbegović is a true hero. He has stood up for his people, spoke out against communism, and went to jail for voicing his opinion.

Izetbegović was born August 8, 1925, in the northern Bosnian town of Bosanski Samac. As soon as he was old enough to take political stands, he spoke out in favor of religious freedom. When only in his early twenties he publicly orated against Yugoslavia's new communist government and its control of religious expression. As a result, he was convicted of rebelling against the government and was jailed from 1946 to 1948.

Izetbegović earned a law degree in 1956 from the University of Sarajevo and became known for his moderate views and his strong condemnation of communism. He earned a living as a consultant for Bosnian companies during most of his legal career, but he stirred up trouble with the communist government again in 1982 when he wrote a book titled *Islam between East and West*. The book described the tenets of the Muslim religion and the difficulties of a Muslim living as a minority in Yugoslavia, a nation with Western values. After the book was released, Izetbegović was convicted of distributing anti-government material and in 1983 was sentenced to 14 years in prison.

An excerpt of the book follows:

> Therefore, to properly understand our position in the world means to submit to God, to find peace, not to start making a more positive effort to encompass and to overcome everything, but rather a negative effort to accept the place and the time of our birth, the place and the time that are our destiny and God's will. Submission to God is the only human and dignified way out of the unsolvable senselessness of life, a way out without revolt, despair, nihilism, or suicide. It

majority of 87 seats in parliament. The Serbian Democratic Party (SDP), headed by Radovan Karadžić (b. 1945), won 72 seats and the Croatian-Democratic Union of Bosnia and Herzegovina (CDU-BH) picked up 44 seats. In total, the three ethnic parties controlled 203 of parliament's 240 total seats.

For the next six months, the presidents of the six Yugoslav republics met frequently. Surely, they thought, there must be some way to keep their nation whole, as a union of six republics. The leaders of Croatia

is a heroic feeling not of a hero, but of an ordinary man who has done his duty and accepted his destiny.

Released early in 1988, Izetbegovic turned his attention to politics as the Yugoslav republic began to weaken. He helped create the Party of Democratic Action. Although it was based on furthering the interests of the Muslim people, the party was dominated by ethnicity as opposed to religion. While Serbs tried to portray him as an extremist who wanted to turn Bosnia into a fundamentalist Islamic nation like Iran, most observers considered him a moderate. In December 1988, he became president of the republic and a soon-to-be new independent nation, Bosnia and Herzegovina.

While the entire region fell into chaos and war from 1992 to 1995, Izetbegović remained in power struggling to do his best for his people. After three years of devastation and genocide, peace negotiations began in late 1995, the year the United Nations celebrated its 50th anniversary. Invited to speak before the UN General Assembly on October 24, 1995, Izetbegović said in part, "We want to create a society based on political and ethnic pluralism, the respect for human rights, and private enterprise. Since, on the other side, everything is opposite to this, we are confident that our ideas will triumph in a peaceful game in the next 5 to 10 years. Thanks to the remarkable superiority of our model of society and state we shall win, with God's help."

A peace treaty signed in 1995 by Izetbegović and the presidents of Serbia and Croatia ended the devastating war. The next year all the citizens of Bosnia and Herzegovina—Muslims, Serbs, and Croats—went to the polls and voted for a new president. Izetbegović was selected to head the nation's three-man presidency. He held the post until June 2000 when he stepped down, citing unfair demands placed by other nations on the Muslims of Bosnia.

and Slovenia favored giving the republics total control over themselves, but as part of a united Yugoslavia. Milošević of Serbia wanted a powerful central Yugoslavian government under Serbian leadership and threatened to annex the parts of Croatia and Bosnia where Serbs were the majority population. Bosnia's Izetbegović and the Macedonians came up with a four-point compromise for preserving Yugoslavia. The presidents of the republics accepted it in principle, but it was never pursued any further.

During a break from these negotiations, Milošević of Serbia and Croatian president Franjo Tudjman had their own secret meeting. Tudjman was a strong nationalist like Milošević. Once elected president of Croatia, he took control of the media and adopted for Croatia a national crest that strongly resembled the flag of the Ustaša—the group that had persecuted Serbs, Jews, and anti-Nazis a half century earlier. This sparked fear among Serbs living in Croatia. It was not long before gun battles between Serbs and Croats broke out in Croatian streets.

Despite the tensions between the Croats and Serbs, the two had a common enemy: Bosnia. At their meeting, Milošević and Tudjman came up with a master plan to divide Bosnia and Herzegovina between their two countries.

Finally, the weakened federal leadership of Yugoslavia simply fell apart. On June 25, Croatia's Tudjman and President Milan Kučan of Slovenia declared their nations' independence from Yugoslavia. Wars immediately broke out between the two republics and what remained of the Yugoslav National Army, now almost entirely controlled by Serbs.

The war in Slovenia lasted just 13 days. With the help of the European Community (EC), a cease fire was declared and a three-month moratorium began on both Croatia and Slovenia's claims of independence. However, before the moratorium ended, the Yugoslav army left Slovenia.

The fighting was more vicious in Croatia. Bosnia became involved since the Yugoslav army used Bosnia as a launching ground for attacks into Croatia. Things became more complicated when the political leader of Bosnia's Serbs, Radovan Karadžić and members of his Serbian Democratic Party, established Serb Autonomous Regions within Bosnia with their own legislatures. In September, the United Nations banned the shipment of weapons to all the former Yugoslav republics; the ban did not stop the illegal flow of weapons into the region. But Bosnia, being surrounded mostly by other republics of Yugoslavia, was unable to take advantage of the unlawful weapon trade. Then, in December, both the Serbs and the Croats living in Bosnia announced they were forming their own separate republics.

On New Year's Day 1992, a cease-fire was declared in Croatia, and, as part of the truce agreement, the United Nations sent members of its United Nations Protection Force (UNPROFOR) to help maintain order.

THE UNITED NATIONS AND THE
UNITED NATIONS PROTECTION FORCE (UNPROFOR)

The United Nations's headquarters are located in New York City. It was founded in 1945, the year World War II ended, with the hope that nations of the world, working out their problems together, could prevent such catastrophic wars.

In the years since, the UN has gotten mixed reviews. Certainly, it has been able to work out some world problems, but it has always had its critics. Currently, some believe that the UN General Assembly, the main group of nations that hears disputes and votes on solutions, is controlled by African and Asian countries, and harbors a prejudice against Israel and the United States.

Regardless, the United Nations is still the only place where the nations of the world meet to solve their disputes. It oversees several agencies and departments aside from the General Assembly that try to make the world a more peaceful and healthier place. These include the UN Children's Fund (UNICEF); the UN Educational, Scientific and Cultural Organization (UNESCO); the World Health Organization (WHO) and for a short time, the United Nations Protection Force (UNPROFOR).

The United Nations Protection Force was the largest, costliest, and most complex peace operation in the UN's history. It was originally headquartered in Sarajevo and had two main goals: to maintain the peace between the groups at war, and to find a permanent solution to the problems of the peoples of the former Yugoslavia. Its forces in March 1995 included 38,599 military personnel.

Although UNPROFOR was originally put into action in Croatia, as the war expanded it was assigned to protect and deliver humanitarian aid to Bosnia and Herzegovina. Its duties included securing Sarajevo's airport and monitoring six "safe areas" established by the UN throughout Bosnia and Herzegovina. UNPROFOR forces were given permission to use force in self-defense in any attacks in those areas. It also was responsible for monitoring cease-fire agreements later in the war. On March 31, 1995, the UN Security Council made a decision to reorganize UNPROFOR and it was replaced with three smaller peacekeeping forces.

At last, on January 15, 1992, the European Community (EC) recognized Slovenia and Croatia as independent countries. Bosnia and Herzegovina also asked for recognition as a separate nation, but was denied the request. The EC said it would recognize Bosnia and Herzegovina only once the status of the Serbs living in the territory was satisfactorily answered.

Bosnia and Herzegovina was by far the most ethnically diverse republic of Yugoslavia. Professor Paul Garde, an expert on the area, breaks down the ethnic population at the time this way: 44 percent Muslims, 31 percent Serbs, and about 17 percent Croats.

Independence

In response, the Bosnian government scheduled a public referendum for February 29 and March 1, 1992. Prior to the referendum, representatives of the three major parties in Bosnia held a meeting in the neutral location of Lisbon, Portugal, where they tried to find a way to prevent the disintegration of Bosnia. The Bosnian Serbs were most concerned. They believed that they would be outvoted by Bosnia's Muslims and Croats since the latter two groups were troubled by the Serbs' aggressive attitude. Under the leadership of Radovan Karadžić, they suggested that Bosnia be divided into smaller self-governing regions rather than an entire homogenous independent republic.

Mate Boban, leader of the Bosnian Croats, agreed right away to this idea. Lacking support from the EC for his idea of an independent Bosnia and Herzegovina, the Muslims' Alija Izetbegović gave his approval as well, feeling this compromise might work. But late in March, the United States announced it supported an independent republic. With the United States behind his original idea. Izetbegović withdrew his support for the compromise solution.

The referendum took place as scheduled and the overwhelming majority of Bosnian Serbs boycotted it. Without the Serbs' votes, it was an easy victory for those in favor of full independence.

However, on March 27 the Bosnian Serbs announced their own constitution and with the support of the Yugoslav People's Army, still a viable force, immediately attacked non-Serb regions of Bosnia. Their aim was to divide Bosnia along ethnic lines and to join the Serb-held areas with Yugoslavia, forming a "greater Serbia." Then, on April 6 the European Community officially recognized the new independent nation of Bosnia-

Herzegovina. At the same time, the republics of Serbia and Montenegro, the only two still governed by communist leaders, formed a new and smaller Federal Republic of Yugoslavia.

Civil War

Just after the European Community recognized Bosnia and Herzegovina as an independent republic, a peace rally took place in downtown Sarajevo. Suddenly the peace demonstrators became targets of machine gun fire. Serbian gunmen had holed themselves up in a Holiday Inn hotel.

The Bosnian Serbs aimed to take over as much of Bosnia as possible, and at first Bosnians and the Croatian Territorial Forces formed a tentative alliance and fought side by side against the Serbs. That association did not last, and soon the Bosnians were fighting the Croats as well as the Serbs.

At the war's outset, the Bosnian government simply wanted to keep firm holds on its major cities and highways. However, Bosnia's military was weak. The Serbs had the mighty Yugoslav People's Army behind them and internally formed a group called the Serbian Volunteer Guard, comprised of terrorist forces.

Serb forces, led by General Ratko Mladić, soon controlled about well over half of Bosnia, including the capital Sarajevo. By destroying highways and controlling the airport, Serbs prevented the people of Sarajevo from getting supplies. A three-year siege of the capital had begun.

The Serbs also employed a controversial type of warfare that became known as ethnic cleansing. The idea of ethnic cleansing was to "clean out" people who belonged to any ethnic group other than one's own, in this case, anyone not of Serbian origin. Bosnian Muslims were tortured and Muslim women were viciously raped in full view of other Muslim citizens. Serbs hoped that Muslim onlookers, fearing for their safety, would flee Bosnia. Thousands were killed, placed in detention camps, or left the country.

The Croats initially fought side by side with the Muslims. The majority of them had supported the idea of an independent and multiethnic Bosnia and Herzegovina, and had voted in the referendum of February 29 and March 1.

The ancient Mostar Bridge stood for more than 400 years, only to be destroyed as a casualty of the Bosnian War on November 9, 1993. (Courtesy United Nations)

However, a group headquartered in western Herzegovina harbored nationalist dreams similar to those of the Bosnian Serbs. They wanted to annex the Croatian section of Bosnia and Herzegovina to their own country, Croatia. The group, headed by Mate Boban, was fully supported by Croatia's president Tudjman. It was Tudjman who in early 1991 had met with Serbian president Milošević and planned to divide Bosnia and Herzegovina between their two countries. By the spring of 1993, the Croats of Bosnia and the Bosnian government were at odds with each other. Each was trying to control the old city of Mostar, the capital of the Herzegovina area.

The fighting between the Bosnians and Croats was brutal, with both peoples proving that the Serbs had no monopoly on ethnic cleansing. Both Bosnians and Croats were guilty of that tactic in Mostar, though never to the degree of the Serbs elsewhere.

The battle continued in Mostar through the rest of 1993. Then on November 9, Croatian soldiers destroyed the Mostar Bridge, made of beautiful white marble, that spanned the Neretva River. It had been built in 1566 by a renowned Ottoman architect named Mimar Hajrudin under the rule of the illustrious Sultan Süleyman the Magnificent. In an instant, war had destroyed it.

The devastation continued. The Croats would destroy a Muslim mosque; in retaliation the Muslims would burn a Catholic church. Muslims in the Bosnian army murdered at least 35 civilians in the town of Križ in September; in October, Croatian forces massacred Muslim villagers in Stupni Do.

The fighting between the Bosnian military and the Serbs did not let up either. On February 5, 1994, 68 civilians who were shopping and talking with neighbors in an outdoor Sarajevo market were killed by a Serb mortar shell and more than 200 civilians were injured. This was reported internationally. Also by this time, television images of starving Muslim war prisoners in Serb-run prison camps in Bosnia had also been broadcast many times across the world. International pressure for peace negotiations increased.

The Trnopolje detention camp, located 175 miles northwest of Sarajevo, was one of several established by Serbs during the Bosnian war. (AP/Wide World Photos/Srdjan Sulja)

Attempts at Peace

Negotiations for a peaceful settlement began in earnest in 1994. In March of that year, Bosnia and Croatia, aided by the United States, agreed to form a Bosniak/Croat federation. But the Serbs continued to fight, ignoring an international peace plan proposed later that year.

Former U.S. president Jimmy Carter initiated a meeting between Bosnia's Serbs and the Bosnian government. They negotiated a four-month long truce that began on New Year's Day, 1995. However, the treaty did not include the people of the Serbian republic, now part of the new Yugoslavia. It did not matter much, since the truce between the Bosnian Serbs and the Bosnian government did not hold.

Some of the bloodiest violence of the war was yet to come. On April 8, Bosnian Serbs attacked airplanes carrying aid to Bosniak war refugees. Concerned that the safety of aid workers was in jeopardy, authorities closed the Sarajevo airport. Then on May 26, the Serbs bombed Sarajevo. Members of the North Atlantic Treaty Organization (NATO), an alliance of the United States, Canada, and most western European countries, responded to the Sarajevo attack, by bombing Serb positions. Bosnian Serbs retaliated by kidnapping and holding more than 350 United Nations peacekeepers hostage. Leaders of the Serbian republic who wanted to improve their relations with the United States and western Europe managed to help negotiate the hostages' release.

Incident at Srebrenica

One hotly contested spot was the city of Srebrenica, about 10 miles from the Serbian border. It had been designated one of several United Nations safe areas, and refugees were being protected there by about 600 members of the Dutch infantry, part of the peacekeeping units. As part of the safe area agreement, the residents of Srebrenica turned over their weapons to the peacekeepers. But by the middle of July the name Srebrenica became synonymous with the worst war massacre in Europe since World War II.

In early summer, Bosnian Serbs laid siege to this safe area of Srebrenica, preventing food from reaching the refugees. On July 6, they shelled the city. They continued their attack on the beleaguered town for days. As the Serbs advanced, they attacked the peacekeepers, taking about 30 hostage. The peacekeeping commander begged the UN headquarters in Sarajevo for air support. At first, they refused, but after a second request, agreed. On July 10, with the threat of air cover imminent, the Serbs stopped their attacks.

As thousands of refugees huddled in fear in Srebrenica the evening of the 10th, the Dutch peacekeepers warned the Serbs that they would still launch air attacks if they did not leave the safe area by six o'clock the next morning.

Six o'clock rolled around and the Serbs had not withdrawn from Srebrenica. NATO aircraft hovered over the town, but because of a silly administrative mistake the air strikes could not begin. Around nine o'clock that morning, the Dutch commander learned that he submitted his request for air backup on a wrong form. A follow-up request on the correct form was sent later that morning.

There was another problem. Since the airplanes had been in the air since 6 A.M., they had to fly to Italy to be refueled. Many of the refugees had fled Srebrenica and gathered just a bit north in a town called Potočari, where a Dutch battalion was based.

After two major delays, two Dutch F-16 fighter planes dropped two bombs on Bosnian Serb units girding Srebrenica. The Serbs threatened to kill both their Dutch hostages and Muslim refugees if the air strikes continued. NATO had no choice but to stop the strikes.

On July 12, the Bosnian Serbs started separating Muslim men over the age of 12 from Muslim women and children. They sent buses to take the women, children, and some sick, elderly men to another safe area in Tuzla, some 35 miles away. The men and older boys, separated from their families, were carted off to warehouses and a soccer stadium.

One Serb witness stated, "The most incredible thing was the silence. It was the silence of pure terror." According to the UN, Serb commander Mladić said the Muslim men were to be questioned about war crimes.

The first unarmed Bosnian Muslims were killed on July 13. Thousands more were murdered the next day. The Dutch peacekeepers had turned over several thousand Muslims to the Serbs in exchange for peacekeepers who were being held hostage. It has been estimated that 7,000 Muslim men and boys—some not even teenagers—were killed at Srebrenica.

On July 21, similar attack on unarmed Bosnian Muslims took place in another designated safe area, the town of Zepa. Then, on August 1, NATO once again threatened air strikes should any more safe areas be attacked.

The fighting continued over the next few months. On August 4, Bosnian Croats began an offensive against Bosnian Serbs and regained the region of Krajina, which the Serbs had held for four years. A week later, the U.S. Congress approved a bill to end the arms embargo on Bosnia. Without the embargo, Bosnian Muslims would be able to acquire weapons legally to fight back against the Serb occupiers. But President Bill Clinton felt that more weapons in the region would expand the war and he vetoed the bill. At the same time he sent U.S. diplomat Richard Holbrooke to the region on a peace mission.

Regardless, the violence continued. On August 28, Bosnian Serbs again shelled a Sarajevo market, killing 37 and injuring 85 people. Both NATO and the UN peacekeepers responded by attacking Serb positions in Bosnia. The Bosnian Serbs agreed to move their weapons from Sarajevo in mid-September and NATO ceased bombing.

Peace, at Last

In early October, President Clinton's peace strategy bore fruit. A cease-fire for Bosnia was announced on October 5 and it went into effect over most of Bosnia a week later. (Some fighting did continue in northwest Bosnia.)

The U.S. mediator Richard Holbrooke traveled to Moscow with other representatives to try to get peace talks to start. From October 16 through October 18 Holbrooke and the other diplomats journeyed to the capitals of the former Yugoslav republics. A decision was reached. Peace negotiations would start on November 1, 1995, at Wright-Patterson Air Force Base in Dayton, Ohio. Aside from Holbrooke, the principle parties in attendance were Bosnia's president Alija Izerbegović, Croatia's president Franjo Tudjman, and Yugoslavia's president Slobodan Milošević, representing the Bosnian Serbs.

Just three weeks later, on November 21, a peace treaty was signed in Dayton. The war was over. Over the course of roughly four years of fighting, a total of 200,000 people had been killed and more than 2 million had been forced out of their homes.

Alija Izetbegović (left), president of Bosnia and Herzegovina, shakes hands with Serbian president Slobodan Milošević (right) as president of Croatia Franjo Tudjman looks on at the Dayton peace talks in Ohio on November 1, 1995. (AP/Wide World Photos/Joe Marquette).

A summary of the lengthy Dayton Peace Agreement (known formally as The General Framework for Peace in Bosnia and Herzegovina) follows:

Bosnia and Herzegovina, Croatia, and the Federal Republic of Yugoslavia [FRY] agree to fully respect the sovereign equality of one another and to settle disputes by peaceful means.

The FRY and Bosnia and Herzegovina recognize each other, and agree to discuss further aspects of their mutual recognition.

The parties agree to fully respect and promote fulfillment of the commitments made in the various Annexes [more specific agreements], and they obligate themselves to respect human rights and the rights of refugees and displaced persons.

The parties agree to cooperate fully with all entities, including those authorized by the United Nations Security Council, in implementing the peace settlement and investigating and prosecuting war crimes and other violations of international humanitarian law.

An addendum to the agreement relates specifically to refugees. It reads in part, "The agreement grants refugees and displaced persons the right to safely return home and regain lost property, or to obtain just compensation."

Among other statements, the parties also agreed to hold free and fair internationally supervised elections and to divide Bosnia and Herzegovina into two separate entities: the Federation of Bosnia and Herzegovina (governed by and home to Bosniaks and Croats) and the Bosnian Serb Republic, known as the Republika Srpska, or RS. They also agreed to establish a constitution providing "for the protection of human rights and the free movement of people, goods, capital and services throughout Bosnia and Herzegovina."

The treaty was signed by Izetbegović, Tudjman, and Milošević in Paris, France, on December 14, 1995. A total of 61,000 peacekeeping troops, called the NATO Implementation Force (IFOR), were sent to the region within a few weeks. The troops were meant to stay for only one year, but officials decided that to maintain the peace it was necessary that they stay for two. In 1997, the forces were cut nearly in half and became known as the Stabilization Force (SFOR).

After the War

For the most part, what many of the world's observers thought was impossible had taken place. Some nay-sayers predicted that peace would not hold and this troubled part of the world would break into war again, but this time with American and European NATO troops fighting as well. They predicted numerous American and European casualties.

That has not happened. The peace has been kept. A Bosnian Serb confessed to American soldiers in 1999, "If you guys weren't here, we'd still be on the front lines." But it has not been easy.

Aside from such major issues as adapting to a new constitution, which was drafted as part of the Dayton Peace Agreement, and aiding the return of thousands of refugees to their homes, trivial problems also needed attention. These included everything from deciding on a design for a national flag to selecting a standard form of currency.

Since then there have been mixed reports on how Bosnia has been faring. Sarajevo has gradually become an operational city, with electricity, running water, and a lively marketplace. However, thousands of refugees have yet to return to their homes. In 1998, Muhamed Sacirbey Bosnia and Herzegovina's UN ambassador said, "We are actually putting Humpty Dumpty back together in some places, but it's a long task."

As participants looked back on the war, they found there was plenty of blame to go around. The United Nations did not hesitate to reprimand itself for the massacre at Srebrenica. In an official report investigating the atrocity, UN secretary-general Kofi Annan announced that the organization used poor judgment, treating the Muslims and Serbs as equal participants when it should have made a " 'moral judgment' that the Serbs' campaign of ethnic cleansing was evil." Annan admitted the United Nations learned from its grave mistake and that safe areas would never again be established without reliable means of defense.

The people and the government of the Netherlands have done much soul searching since the Srebrenica massacre, and the entire Dutch

The process of reconstruction is a long, expensive one. Workers in this photo repair a damaged house in Sarajevo in December 1999. (AP/Wide World Photos/Hidajet Delic)

UNITED NATIONS WAR CRIMES TRIBUNAL

Early in the war, when reports of ethnic cleansing were beginning to filter out into the rest of the world, the United Nations decided something had to be done. On May 25, 1993, the UN Security Council passed Resolution 827 establishing the International Criminal Tribunal for the Former Yugoslavia. It is the first international body for the prosecution of war crimes since the end of World War II, when similar courts took place in Nuremberg, Germany, and Tokyo, Japan.

Based in The Hague, the de jure capital of the Netherlands, the tribunal has jurisdiction for persons accused of war crimes, crimes against humanity, and genocide in former Yugoslavia occurring since January 1, 1991. The tribunal does not maintain a police force; arrests are made by police in the former Yugoslav republics, other states, or international peace forces such as the Stabilization Force.

According to rules imposed by the UN Security Council, the tribunal may not impose the death penalty as punishment. In order to increase the chances of a fair trial, suspects are not allowed to be tried in absentia. Some suspected war criminals have escaped and cannot be tried as long as they are at large.

By February 2002, there was a total of 19 guilty verdicts and two acquittals. Then on July 31, 2003, the stiffest sentence so far was meted out. A former Bosnian Serb mayor, Milomir Stakić, was found guilty of extermination, murder, and persecution for his role in setting up detention camps in northwest Bosnia where more than 1,500 non-Serbs were murdered and 20,000 deported. Stakić was the first person given a life sentence by The Hague tribunal.

cabinet resigned in April 2002 in response to a report that blamed the government for failing to prevent the massacre. Many Dutch people are ashamed of their soldiers' inability to prevent the event, but there is considerable debate over whether, given the limitations on their peacekeeping forces, anything could have realistically been done.

Credit has also been given where it is due. On November 19, 1999, President Bill Clinton was awarded the first annual Dayton Peace Prize for his role in ending the Bosnian war. Prominent peace broker Richard Holbrooke praised Clinton, stating, "To deploy those troops was a very bold political move," considering the decision was made less than a year before the 1996 presidential election when Clinton was running for a second term, and when 70 percent of the American public was against it.

As the 21st century got under way, so did a United Nations War Crimes Tribunal in The Hague, Netherlands, where Serbian war leaders, including former Yugoslav president Slobodan Milošević, were put on trial for war crimes. Then, on July 15, 2002, the presidents of Bosnia and Herzegovina, Croatia, and Yugoslavia met for the first time since the Dayton Peace Agreement had been signed almost seven years earlier. It seemed that the situation in the former Yugoslavia was getting somewhat back to normal.

Around the same time, the people of Mostar began the long task of building an exact replica of the historic bridge over the Neretva River destroyed by a Croat shell nine years earlier. Emil Balić, a Mostar resident and competitive diver who had jumped many times from the bridge as part of diving meets, said he saw the bridge as a symbol of life getting back to normal. He commented, "People will at least gather around the bridge and talk again. Time will help us reconcile. . . . I live to see the arch again."

NOTES

p. 35 "'It was the first time, and . . .'" "Sarajevo, Yugoslavia: 1984," Washington Post. Available on-line. URL: http://www.washingtonpost.com/wp-srv/sports/longterm/olympics1998/history/years/1984.htm. Downloaded August 29, 2002.

p. 35 "A total of 49 nations . . ." "Sarajevo, Yugoslavia: 1984," Washington Post.

p. 37 "But in 1989 alone . . ." Robert J. Donia and John V. A. Fine, Jr. *Bosnia and Herzegovina: A Tradition Betrayed* (New York: Columbia University Press, 1994), p. 199.

p. 39 "By 1990, roughly 40 percent . . ." Donia and Fine, p. 186.

p. 40 "The Serbian Democratic Party (SDP) . . ." "The Story of Bosnia-Herzegovina." Available on-line. URL: http://bosniak.netfirms.com/research/bosnia.herzegovina.html. Downloaded August 31, 2002.

pp. 40–41 "'Therefore, to properly understand . . .'" Alija Izetbegović, "Submission to God." Available on-line. URL: http://www.angelfire.com/dc/mbooks/izetbegovic.html. Downloaded August 30, 2002.

p. 41 "'We want to create a society based on . . .'" "Statement by H.E. President Alija Izetbegovic, The Republic of Bosnia and Herzegovina, Special Commemorative Meeting of the General Assembly on the occasion of the Fiftieth Anniversary of the United Nations, October 24, 1995, New York." Available on-line. URL: http://www.cco.caltech.edu/~bosnia/embassy/un1024.html. Downloaded August 30, 2002.

p. 43 "The United Nations Protection Force was the largest . . ." Igor Ilic and Slavoljob Leko, "UNPROFOR Facts and Figures." Available on-line. URL: http://www.hr/hrvatska/WAR/UNPF-facts.html. Downloaded September 11, 2002.

p. 43 "Its forces in March 1995 . . ." Department of Public Information, United Nations, "Former Yugoslavia-UNPROFOR." Available on-line. URL: http://www.un.org/Depts/DPKO/Missions/unprof_p.htm. Downloaded September 11, 2002.

p. 44 "Bosnia and Herzegovina was by far . . ." "An Expert's Overview." Available on-line. URL: http://www.pbs.org/wgbh/pages/frontline/shows/karadzic/bosnia/bosnia.html. Downloaded September 13, 2002.

p. 47 "Muslims in the Bosnian army . . ." Donia and Fine, p. 256.

p. 47 "On February 5, 1994, 68 civilians . . ." Donia and Fine, p. 268.

p. 49 "'The most incredible thing . . .'" Bruce W. Nelan, "Tears and Terror." Available on-line. URL: http://www.time.com/time/europe/eu/printout/0,9689,168098,00.html. Downloaded September 13, 2002.

p. 49 "According to the UN, . . ." Nelan, "Tears and Terror."

p. 49 "It has been estimated that . . ." "World Europe Srebrenica Report Blames UN," November 16, 1999. Available on-line. URL: http://news.bbc.co.uk/1/hi/world/europe/521825.stm. Downloaded September 13, 2002.

pp. 50–51 "Over the course of roughly . . ." "Bosnian Leaders Embrace New Era," July 15, 2002. Available on-line. URL: http://news.bbc.co.uk/2/hi/europe/2128641.stm. Downloaded September 14, 2002.

pp. 51–52 "'Bosnia and Herzegovina, Croatia, and the . . .'" "U.S. Department of State: Summary of the Dayton Peace Agreement on Bosnia-Herzegovina: Fact Sheet Released by the Office of the Spokesman, November 30, 1995." Available on-line. URL: http://www.state.gov/www/regions/eur/bosnia/bossumm.html. Downloaded September 13, 2002.

p. 52 "'for the protection of human rights . . .'" "U.S. Department of State: Summary of the Dayton Peace Agreement."

p. 52 "A total of 61,000 . . ." "NATO Implementation Force (IFOR)." Available on-line. URL: http://www.stratnet.ucalgary.ca/elearning/module1/readings/ifor.htm. Downloaded January 10, 2003.

p. 52 "'If you guys weren't here . . .'" "A Few Good Men in Bosnia," March 17, 1999. Available on-line. URL: http://www.cbsnews.com/stories/1999/03/17/eveningnews/printable39321.shtml. Downloaded September 13, 2002.

p. 53 "'We are actually putting . . .'" "Bosnia Remains Deeply Divided," April 29, 1998. Available on-line. URL: http://www.cbsnews.com/stories/1998/04/29/world/printable8352.shtml. Downloaded September 13, 2002.

p. 53 "'"moral judgment" that the Serbs' campaign . . .'" "U.N. Admits Bosnia Blunders," November 16, 1999. Available on-line. URL: http://www.cbsnews.com/stories/1999/11/16/world/printable70520.shtml. Downloaded September 13, 2002.

p. 54 "'To deploy those troops . . .'" "Clinton Receives Dayton Peace Prize," November 17, 2000. Available on-line. URL: http://www.cbsnews.com/stories/2000/11/17/world/printable250442.shtml. Downloaded September 14, 2002.

p. 54 "By February 2002, there . . ." "War Crimes Tribunal: Key Facts," February 14, 2002. Available on-line. URL: http://www.cnn.com/2001/WORLD/europe/11/23/tribunal.key.facts. Downloaded January 8, 2003.

p. 55 " 'People will at last . . .' " Andrew Purvis, "Across the Great Divide." Available on-line. URL: http://www.time.com/time/europe/magazine/printout/0,13155,901020729-322608,00.html. Downloaded September 13, 2002.

PART II
Bosnia and Herzegovina Today

4

GOVERNMENT

〜⌇〜

Today the citizens of Bosnia and Herzegovina live in an emerging democracy. After decades of being governed by a president-for-life in a one-party system, and after four years of civil war, Bosnians will need time to get used to a free government.

Yet, many experts say Bosnia and Herzegovina is progressing more smoothly than they could have imagined in 1995 when the Dayton Peace Agreement was signed.

Unlike the United States, Canada, or many countries in western Europe, Bosnia and Herzegovina is neither an ethnic melting pot nor a cultural mosaic. The civil war has left a constant tension between Serbs, Bosniaks, and Croats; this presents a challenge to the Dayton Peace Agreement, which declares that the new government must be both democratic and multiethnic.

Two Divisions

The fairest way to achieve this was to divide the nation into two parts. One is the Bosniak/Croat Federation of Bosnia and Herzegovina (the Federation, for short), controlled by Bosniaks, or Bosnian Muslims, and Croats. The other is Republika Srpska (RS), also known as the Serb Republic (SR), which is governed by Serbs.

The exception is the community of Brčko, located in northeastern Bosnia. It is a self-governing administrative unit and not part of the Federation or the RS. The unique situation of Brčko will be discussed later in the chapter.

The Federation covers 51 percent of the nation. The RS occupies the other 49 percent. Overseeing both units is a central presidency, which appoints a federal Council of Ministers.

An Unusual Presidency

The presidency is actually a co-presidency. Unlike most other nations, three people form the head of state of Bosnia and Herzegovina. One Bosniak and one Croat are elected directly by the citizens of the Federation, and a third member, a Serb, is elected by the people of the RS. Each is elected for a four-year term, but as was done in the post-Tito years of Yugoslavia in the 1980s, they rotate holding the position of president every eight months. The candidate who receives the most votes serves as chairman of the presidency.

The presidency is in charge of conducting Bosnia and Herzegovina's foreign policy, appointing ambassadors and the nation's other international representatives, representing the country in international organizations, and negotiating treaties. One responsibility of the president—unrelated to foreign policy—is executing the recommendations of a second governmental body, the Council of Ministers.

This council is nominated by the presidency, but must be confirmed by the House of Representatives. The House of Representatives and the smaller House of Peoples together form the Parliamentary Assembly.

The Council of Ministers is responsible for carrying out the nation's policies, and reports to the Parliamentary Assembly.

Members of the Council of Ministers include

1. two co–prime ministers and one deputy prime minister
2. a minister and two deputy ministers for foreign affairs
3. a minister and two deputy ministers for foreign trade and economic relations
4. a minister and two deputy ministers for civil affairs and communications

The second branch of government, the Parliamentary Assembly's two houses, are divided to permit equal representation for all the citizens of Bosnia and Herzegovina.

Members of the House of Representatives are elected directly by the people. There is a total of 42 members in the house, with two-thirds, or 28 people, elected directly from the more populous Federation and one-third, or 14 members, from the Republika Srpska.

The House of Peoples has 15 members, equally divided with five Bosniaks, five Croats, and five Serbs. Unlike the House of Representatives, members of this smaller chamber are not elected directly. The Bosniaks and Croats are chosen by the Bosniak and Croat delegates to the House of Representatives. The Serbs are picked by the National Assembly of the Serb Republic. All members of the Parliamentary Assembly serve two-year terms.

Three members take turns as chairpersons of each body and, as one might expect, the group of chairpersons is comprised of representatives from each ethnic group. The Parliamentary Assembly, which meets in the national capital of Sarajevo, makes laws, approves or disapproves specific treaties shared between Bosnia and Herzegovina and other countries, and prepares a national budget.

The third branch of the federal government is the Bosnia and Herzegovina Constitutional Court. It consists of nine judges, but it is composed differently from the presidency and legislature. A total of four of the nine judges are chosen by the Federation's House of Representatives, while two are selected by the RS's National Assembly. The other three are non-Bosnians, picked by the president of the European Court of Human Rights, after consulting with the Bosnian presidency. Judges are appointed for five-year terms.

Government on the local level works similarly, but on a smaller scale. The Federation of Bosnia and Herzegovina and the Republika Srpska have their own three-pronged systems of government, with executive, legislative, and judicial branches.

The Federation has its own president and vice president, while its legislature consists of a House of Representatives and a House of Nations. The judicial system is comprised of numerous courts. These include a Constitutional Court, a Supreme Court, and a Human Rights Court. The Federation is divided into 10 smaller divisions, called cantons.

The Serb Republic, or Republika Srpska, is governed by a president and two vice presidents, while its legislature consists of just one body, the 82-member House of Representatives. Like the Federation, the SR has several individual courts including a Constitutional Court, a Supreme Court, basic, and district courts. Both the Federation and SR's governments include several ministries, just like the federal government.

The Problem of Brčko

Brčko is situated in a vulnerable location. It is just across the Bosnian border from the Vojvodina district of Serbia in the current nation of Serbia and Montenegro, and also very close to the border of Croatia. As such, it falls outside this government structure. As the transportation, industry, and trade center of the region, Brčko is a very important community.

It was not until four years after the Dayton Accords were signed that a solution to the Brčko problem was approved. At the original peace talks in 1995, none of the negotiators could agree on who would control Brčko. Rather than delay the rest of the treaty, the Brčko question was postponed for one year.

A committee was formed in 1996 to tackle this issue. Richard Holbrooke, chief negotiator of the Dayton treaty, was not involved this time. However, a legal scholar who had worked with the Holbrooke team, Roberts Owen, took Holbrooke's place as the main negotiator. The two units of Bosnia and Herzegovina each nominated a mediator to represent their people. The Federation chose a professor named Čazim Sadiković while the RS selected another professor, Vitomar Popović.

The original goal was to make a decision about Brčko by December 14, 1996, exactly one year after the Dayton Peace Agreement was signed in Paris. However, there were still complex problems involved in carrying out the basics of Dayton, so it was decided to postpone a solution to Brčko once again. Interim laws were put in place until a permanent answer could be worked out.

The first official decision regarding Brčko was made by the committee, formally called the Arbitration Tribunal, at a meeting in Rome, Italy, on February 14, 1997. The city was placed under international supervision with a supervisor (the deputy high representative) in a complete position of authority, overseeing the implementation of the Dayton Accords. The first deputy high representative was U.S. Ambassador Robert W. Farrand, who arrived in Brčko on April 11, 1997. His position had several objectives, including:

1. To help refugees from Brčko return to their original homes in an orderly manner.
2. To promote a democratic government and a multiethnic administration in Brčko.
3. To guarantee freedom of movement for the residents, and to help bring normal policing functions to Brčko.
4. To work with border officials in order to help customs procedures and controls proceed smoothly.
5. To help revive Brčko's economy.

A little more than a year later, the tribunal met again and reaffirmed their 1997 decision. At the same time it warned the Republika Srpska that it needed to show "significant new achievements in terms of returns of former Brčko residents." The tribunal stressed that while the Federation did not have the same responsibility regarding refugees and Brčko, it too, had to allow former residents to return to their homes in all parts of the Federation, especially in Sarajevo.

It was not until 1999 that a final decision regarding Brčko was made. For 10 days the Arbitration Tribunal heard testimony from all parties involved. The final report, issued on March 5, 1999, stated that Brčko would be a special district, under the sovereignty of the nation of Bosnia and Herzegovina.

At the same time it would belong to both the Federation and the SR. However, Brčko would govern itself with "a single, unitary, multiethnic, democratic Government; a unified and multiethnic police force operating under a single command structure as an independent judiciary." It was also to be demilitarized. Brčko would not have its own flag but would fly the flags of both the Federation and the RS.

At the time, U.S. secretary of state Madeleine K. Albright announced,

Looking back over the past year, I do not see how any other decision could have been made or any reason for its delay. Today is an important day for the people of Bosnia and marks the close of the last outstanding territorial question left open at Dayton.

The Dayton Agreement gave to the Arbitrator absolute authority to resolve the issue of Brvcko. I know the leaders of both parties, as well as Presidents Milovsevi´c and Tudjman, supported the choice of Roberts Owen as the Arbitrator and personally committed themselves to implementing the decision when made. I call upon them to fulfill that commitment. . . .

The decision respects the interests of both entities and all Bosnia's people, and provides a real opportunity to see Brvcko become an example of reconciliation and progress . . . I praise Mr. Owen for his personal commitment, fairness and wisdom. It now again falls to the people of Bosnia to ensure a peaceful and prosperous future.

Political Parties

Bosnia and Herzegovina has many political parties that represent many views, from the most liberal on the left to the most conservative on the right. In addition, some parties are active only in one of the two national districts, while others maintain a presence in the entire country. Regardless, the majority of political parties in Bosnia and Herzegovina are based primarily on ethnicity.

For example, the Party of Democratic Action (SDA) is the leading Muslim party. It was founded in 1990 by Alija Izetbegović, the man who became president, an Islamic scholar, and a diplomat named Haris Siladžić. Originally it was a multiethnic group, but in time became mainly an ethnic Muslim party. Most observers view it as a nationalist Muslim party, whose rank-and-file membership consists of radicals and moderates. On political and economic matters, the SDA supports a strong central government, while asserting the right of each ethnic group in Bosnia and Herzegovina to continue to celebrate their own cultural heritage without governmental interference.

The SDA's chief opponent is the Bosnian Social Democratic Party (SDP), which was formed on February 27, 1999, with the merger of two smaller democratic social parties, the Social Democrats of BiH and the Social Democratic Party of BiH. The SDP's leanings are non-nationalistic.

The Serb Democratic Party (SDS) has a singular purpose: to look out for the welfare of all Serbs. While founded as an ultra-nationalist party, today it contains both moderate and ultra-nationalist wings. The ultra-nationalists of this party supported strongman and co-founder Radovan Karadžić. Once Karadžić was indicted for war crimes during the Bosnian War, the SDS moderates forced him to resign. Under international pressure, the SDS voted in 2001 to expel all those suspected of war crimes.

Two other Serbian parties are active in Bosnia and Herzegovina's national politics, and both have ultra-nationalist leanings. One is the Serb Radical Party of the Serb Republic (SRS SR), founded by Vojislav Šešelj, another indicted war criminal from the Bosnian War. For a long time SRS SR wanted to form a united Serbia and to have the Bosnian district of Srpska universally recognized as its own independent nation. Šešelj went on to become the deputy prime minister of the current nation of Yugoslavia. Under new party leader, Nikola Poplašen, the SRS SR, still considered ultra-nationalist, toned down its demands for a united Serbia.

A much smaller but more nationalistic political organization is the Serbian Unity Party (SSJ). The SSJ strongly believes that Bosnia's Srpska district should be part of the Federal Republic of Yugoslavia, and one of the party's most active members was Željko Ražnatović, who was known during the Bosnian War by the alias, Arkan. Arkan and his followers were directly involved in ethnic cleansing and he was also indicted as a war criminal.

The Croats, too, have several parties, but the most significant is the Croatian Democratic Community of Bosnia and Herzegovina (HDZ BiH). It was founded by the president of Croatia, Franjo Tudjman, and continues to be closely—but unofficially—tied to the Croats in Croatia. The HDZ BiH also has nationalist tendencies, although they can vary in degree depending on who is the leader at any given moment. Just about all members of the HDZ BiH favor some kind of stronger autonomy for the Croats of Bosnia. While some want to become part of a greater nation of Croatia, others simply wish to have more independence from the Bosniaks.

Of the many parties in the Federation, one of the most prominent is the Party for Bosnia Herzegovina (SBiH). It was the brainchild of both founders of the SDA, Alija Izetbegović, and Haris Silajdažić, who founded it in April 1996. Silajdažić, the party's kingpin, hoped that it would be a welcome home for both the Muslims and Croats living in the

BERIZ BELKIĆ

Beriz Belkić is the most moderate chairman of the presidency of Bosnia and Herzegovina since Alija Izetbegović held office. Born on September 8, 1946, in Sarajevo, Belkić was raised and went to college in the nation's historic capital, graduating with a degree in economics.

Belkić spent the Bosnian War as defense secretary of the Bosnian municipality of Ilidža, and then from 1996 to 1998 he held a government post with a cumbersome title—minister for labor, social policy, displaced persons and refugees in the government in the Canton of Sarajevo—but with a direct relation to the reconstruction of his country. He was then elected as a delegate of the assembly of the canton of Sarajevo and the counselor of the municipality of Novo Sarajevo.

In November 2000 he was elected to his first national position: member of the House of Representatives of the Parliamentary Assembly. Then, on March 30, 2001, voters chose him to be a member of the Presidency of Bosnia and Herzegovina. He became chairman on February 14, 2002.

On May 13, 2002, he spoke at the United Nations in New York City, on the massacre at Srebrenica, at the Srebrenica Regional Recovery Programme Donor Conference. In it he urged member nations of the UN to use their financial resources to "bring life back to this region, to help the people there build a self-sustainable and happy community."

Belkić spoke from his heart when he stated,

> Today I most probably have the most difficult task in my life. I am supposed to convey to you the message of the survivors from the Srebrenica region. A message from people who survived one of the greatest civilization tragedies of the last century.
>
> Srebrenica is the shame of the modern international system, of modern civilization. . . . It is hard, and I am afraid it might be impossible, to speak today on behalf of those who lost their dearest,

Federation. And while Croats are invited to join, the party membership consists mainly of Bosnian Muslims.

The Croatian Peasants' Party (HSS) might have the word "Croatian" in its official title, but it is a centrist party that strongly supports a united Bosnia and Herzegovina. Like the Party for Bosnia Herzegovina, anybody can join the HSS, although most of its members are Croatians of north-central Bosnia.

who, for years, have been searching for missing children, fathers, mothers, brothers and sisters, who have lost everything they had. . . .

The people of the Srebrenica region see a chance in this programme, the start of caring and consideration for them. . . . They are prepared to take the responsibility for the realization of the programme with the necessary help of the state and entity authorities in Bosnia and Herzegovina and experts of the UN development Programme.

TRENDS

The United States and western Europe have been hoping for a moderate trend in Bosnian politics since the war. They have not always gotten their way. Since Bosnia is a democracy whose people directly elect their leaders, all other nations can do is sit on the sidelines and observe.

In elections in 2000 and 2002 nationalistic parties won significant victories. In 2000, the extremist Croat party, HDZ, and the similarly ultra-nationalistic Serb party, SDS, received substantial numbers of votes. The Bosniak vote between the nationalist SDA and the non-nationalist SDP was close, but in March 2001 the SDP was allowed to form a government, replacing the SDA, which had been in power for the previous decade.

Having lost ground to more moderate parties, and using the election as a pretext, Bosnia's Croat National Assembly rejected the SDP government and declared self-rule. The international civilian agency charged with implementing and overseeing the peace settlement, the Office of the High Representative (OHR), responded by removing Croat leader Ante Jelavić as a member of the Bosnian presidency and head of the HDZ. Over the course of 2001, the OHR regularly removed from office nationalistic leaders it considered to be obstructionist.

Other centrist and moderate parties in the Federation include the Civil Democratic Party (GDS); the Republican Party (Republikanski); the Croatian Democratic Union, (HDZ), which was founded by a pro-Croat and anti-Izetbegović Muslim named Fikret Abdić, who was also indicted as a war criminal; and the Bosniak Organization (BO), which actually started out as a somewhat Muslim nationalist organization but has since become much more moderate.

OFFICE OF THE HIGH REPRESENTATIVE

The brokers of the Dayton Peace Agreement felt that an impartial post should be established to make certain that all aspects of the treaty were properly carried out. The High Representative is the final authority regarding the interpretation of the agreement and is duly authorized to make a wide range of decisions, from imposing legislation to removing obstructive leaders.

Article I and II of the framework agreement follow:

> 1. The Parties agree that the implementation of the civilian aspects of the peace settlement will entail a wide range of activities including continuation of the humanitarian aid effort for as long as necessary; rehabilitation of infrastructure and economic reconstruction; the establishment of political and constitutional institutions in Bosnia and Herzegovina; promotion of respect for human rights and the return of displaced persons and refugees; and the holding of free and fair elections according to the timetable in Annex 3 to the General Framework Agreement. A considerable number of international organizations and agencies will be called upon to assist.
>
> 2. In view of the complexities facing them, the Parties request the designation of a High Representative, to be appointed consis-

The most successful party in the Republika Srpska has traditionally been the Serbian People's Union (SNS). It was started by Biljana Plavšić, a former disciple of war criminal Radovan Karadžić. At first Plavšić publicly dissociated herself from Karadžić. However, on October 2, 2002, she pleaded guilty before the International Criminal Tribunal for the Former Yugoslavia to the charge of crimes against humanity for her role in the 1992–95 war. She expressed "full and unconditional remorse for the harm that was done to innocent victims of the conflict."

The Serbian Civic Council (SGV), another party in the RS, was founded to protect the rights of Serbs who live in the Federation. Unlike nationalist parties such as the SDS, SRS SR, and SSJ, this party aims to keep the current nation of Bosnia and Herzegovina as it is by helping Bosnian Serbs who resided in the Federation to return to their original homes.

tent with relevant United Nations Security Council resolutions, to facilitate the Parties' own efforts and to mobilize and, as appropriate, coordinate the activities of the organizations and agencies involved in the civilian aspects of the peace settlement by carrying out, as entrusted by a UN Security Council resolution, the tasks set out below.

The Peace Implementation Council (PIC), an organization of 55 countries and international groups that sponsor and direct the peace implementation process, chooses the high representative. A PIC steering committee nominates the high representative, and that person is then endorsed by the United Nations Security Council. The high representative has no authority over the NATO-led military Stabilization Force (SFOR).

There have been four high representatives to date. The first was former Swedish prime minister Carl Bildt (December 1995–June 1997), who was the European Union's special negotiator at the end of the war. Next were former Spanish secretary of state for European affairs Carlos Westendorp (June 1997–July 1999), and former European Union negotiator at the Kosovo peace talks Wolfgang Petritsch (August 1999–May 2002). The current high representative who took his post in May 2002, is the former leader of the Liberal Democratic Party in Great Britain, Paddy Ashdown.

Other parties in the RS include the Social Liberal Party (SLS) which was created as an anti- Karadžić political movement, and the Socialist Party of Republika Srpska (SPRS), which began as an ultra-nationalist party but has become more moderate over the last several years.

Several parties have formed multiparty coalitions in order to gain the most power possible. The most successful of these has been the Coalition for a Unified and Democratic Bosnia and Herzegovina (KCD). It is comprised of members of the SDA, the SDS, and the Party for Bosnia and Herzegovina. The KCD has won numerous seats in the Parliamentary Assembly.

Members of several of the parties, even those based in the two districts, have served as chairman of the presidency. Alija Izetbegović of the SDA was chairman twice, from October 5, 1996, to October 13, 1998, and from February 14 to October 14, 2000. Another chairman, in two

A Bosnian man walks past a campaign poster urging people to vote for the Party of Bosnia Herzegovina, in downtown Sarajevo, in October 2002. Pictured second from the right is chairman of the Bosnian presidency, Beriz Belkić. (AP/Wide World Photos/ Hidajet Delic)

nonconsecutive terms, was Živko Radišić of the Socialist Party (SPRS) of Republika Srpska. He served from October 13, 1998, to June 15, 1999, and October 14, 2000, to June 14, 2001. The first chairman of the presidency from the moderate Party for Bosnia and Herzegovina (SBiH) is Beriz Belkić, who assumed office in 2002 (see sidebar on pp. 68–69).

The federal elections in 2002 showed even stronger support for nationalistic parties. Dragan Ćović, nominee from the nationalist HDZ-BiH, and Serb nationalist, Mirko Šarović, easily won victories. The Bosniak vote was much closer, with Sulejman Tihić of the SDA barely beating former prime minister, Haris Silajdžić, 38 percent to 34 percent.

Immediately, Western leaders expressed concern that the election results indicated a trend toward the ultra-nationalistic policies—the same policies that precipitated the war of the 1990s. High Representative Paddy Ashdown tried to calm those fears. He pointed out that the vote was a response to the nation's high unemployment rate—about 60 percent, in some poor areas—and other economic problems.

Ashdown said, "Everyone who thinks the mood is moving back to nationalism simply has not been listening. The weekend vote was a protest . . . a cry for help, not a vote for more of the same or a return of the past."

Ashdown continued, "Let's wait and see. I would judge these people on what they do in the future. Justice and jobs will be the acid test for the future government."

NOTES

p. 65 " 'significant new achievements . . .' " "History and mandate of the OHR North/Brčko," August 28, 2001. Available on-line. URL: http://www.ohr.int/ print/?content_id+5531. Downloaded September 18, 2002.

p. 65 " 'a single, unitary, multiethnic, democratic Government . . .' " "History and mandate of the OHR North/Brčko." Downloaded September 18, 2002.

pp. 65–66 " 'Looking back over the past . . .' " "Disputed Bosnian Town to Be Run by All Ethnic Groups," CNN, March 5, 1999. Available on-line. URL: http://www.cnn.com/WORLD/europe/9903/05/bosnia.town/index.html. Downloaded October 4, 2002.

p. 68 " 'bring life back to this region . . .' " "Statement of Beriz Belkic, President of BiH Presidency, at the Srebrenica Regional Recovery Programme Donor Conference, UN Headquarters in New York, May 13, 2002." Available on-line. URL: http://www.unmibh.org/stories/view.asp?Story1D-142. Downloaded September 18, 2002.

pp. 68–69 " 'Today I most probably have . . .' " "Statement of Beriz Belkic, President of BiH Presidency, at the Srebrenica Regional Recovery Programme Donor Conference, UN Headquarters in New York, May 13, 2002."

p. 70 " 'full and unconditional . . .' " "Guilty Plea by Former Bosnian Serb Leader Biljana Plavšić," U.S. Department of State website, October 3, 2002. Available on-line. URL: http://www.state.gov/r/pa/prs/ps/2002/14101pf.htm. Downloaded December 28, 2002.

pp. 70–71 " '1. The Parties agree that . . .' " "The General Framework Agreement: Annex 10," December 14, 1995. Available on-line. URL: http://www.ohr.int/ print/?content_id=366. Downloaded January 9, 2003.

p. 72 "The Bosniak vote was much closer . . ." "Ex-PM loses Bosnia Muslim vote," CNN. Available on-line. URL: http://www.cnn.com/2002/WORLD/europe/ 10/09/bosnia.vote/index.html. Downloaded January 9, 2003.

p. 72 "He pointed out that the vote . . ." "Ex-PM Loses Bosnia Muslim vote."

pp. 72–73 " 'Everyone who thinks . . .' " "Ex-PM Loses Bosnia Muslim vote."

5

RELIGION

In Bosnia and Herzegovina, people's religion is not just what they believe, it is also who they are. Their religion affects their identity, how they live and who they vote for.

The main religion in Bosnia and Herzegovina is Islam, which is practiced by about 44 percent of the population. The next most common faith practiced by 31 percent of people is Eastern Orthodox Christianity and the third major religion practiced by 15 percent is Roman Catholicism. Some Protestants and Jews exist, but they number less than 5 percent of the population.

The Muslims are for the most part Bosniaks, or descendants of Bosnians who converted to Islam when the Ottoman Empire was in power. The Eastern Orthodox are mostly Serbs; Croats constitute the vast majority of Catholics. Although all three ethnicities have the same southern Slavic roots, when the Bosniaks have a dispute with the Serbs, for example, it is also a dispute between Muslims and Orthodox Christians.

However, there is also another way to look at the religious diversity. Over the centuries there have been many more periods of peace than war in this Balkan region, in spite of the presence of three dominant religions. For a long time, and even now to a degree, there has been a remarkable acceptance of different religions. It may be an uneasy tolerance, but it is greater than one would find in many other nations with such a diverse multicultural population.

To understand the relationship between the different religions in this country, one must understand each religion as well as the region's long and complex history.

In the seventh century, the prophet Muhammad founded Islam in the city of Mecca, in what is now the sheikdom of Saudi Arabia. Muslims believe in one god named Allah, which means "The God." The Islamic holy book is the Qur'an, also spelled Koran. The Qur'an and the Sunna, which explains the words and practices of Muhammad, form the basis of Islamic law. Muslims practice five pillars of worship: prayer; *shahada,* or the acceptance and confirmation of Allah as the one and only God; alms-giving, or helping the poor; fasting, which Muslims practice from sunrise to sunset everyday during Ramadan, the ninth month of the Islamic calendar; and *hadj,* or pilgrimage, since the Qur'an commands all physically and financially healthy Muslims to make a journey to Mecca.

In general, Muslims believe in respecting their parents and elders, being kind to people and animals, and helping those less fortunate than they are. Muslims believe Islam is a continuation of the teachings of all prophets since the time of Abraham. While a militant and violent form of fundamentalist Islam has been growing strong in much of the Arab world (and in other countries such as Iran and Pakistan), this has not been the case in Bosnia and Herzegovina.

Roman Catholicism dates to around A.D. 30 when Jesus told his apostles to spread his teachings of the Kingdom of God. Roman Catholics believe devoutly in one God, but that the one God takes the form of three entities: the Father, the Son (who is Jesus Christ, or the Messiah), and the Holy Spirit. Jesus, they say, was crucified but rose from the dead and sent the Holy Spirit to guide his apostles. They believe Jesus founded the church to bring salvation to all people. The head of the Roman Catholic Church is the pope, who resides in Vatican City, an independent nation surrounded by Rome, Italy. The pope is considered Jesus Christ's representative on Earth.

There are seven sacraments of the Roman Catholic Church, known collectively as the liturgy. The principle act is the Eucharist, or Mass. According to the Catholic faith, Jesus Christ is literally present during Mass, and He forgives the congregants' sins. The other sacraments are baptism, in which a baby (or adult who is converting) is cleansed of sin and admitted into the Catholic community; confirmation, or becoming a spiritual adult; penance, or the confession of sins; holy orders, in which Catholics become religious leaders; marriage; and anointing of the sick so that they can heal and also receive the grace of the Holy Spirit.

Like all the other Christian denominations, Eastern Orthodox Christianity is an offshoot of Roman Catholicism. It can be traced to the fourth century when Roman emperor Constantine the Great converted to Christianity and relocated his capital to a city he named after himself: Constantinople (today Istanbul, Turkey).

Over the next several centuries, the Eastern, or Constantinopolitan Church and the Catholic Church in Rome had numerous fallings out. One major difference was that the Eastern Orthodox Christians do not believe the pope in Rome should be the authority over the entire religion. In 1054, the eastern and western churches officially split, an incident known as the Great Schism. Aside from a difference in doctrine called the Nicene Creed, not accepting the pope as Jesus' representative on earth is the primary difference between the Catholic and Eastern Orthodox Churches. However, the latter adheres to virtually the same seven sacraments as the Roman Catholic Church.

Technically, there are several Eastern Orthodox Churches and they are primarily located in eastern Europe and western Asia. It is common for them to be called by the nation in which they are located, such as Russian Orthodox and Greek Orthodox. In Bosnia and Herzegovina, they are Serbian Orthodox.

Jews constitute one of the sizable minorities in Bosnia and Herzegovina. Judaism is the oldest of the world's major religions. It was the first religion to practice monotheism, or the belief in one God, and both Christianity and Islam have their bases in Judaism. Jews believe that human beings are created in the image of God and therefore are to be treated with kindness and respect.

The Jews have two holy books. One is the first five books of the Bible: Genesis, Exodus, Leviticus, Numbers, and Deuteronomy. Together, these are called the Torah, and they form the basis of all Jewish beliefs. The other is the Talmud, which consists of writings that elaborate Jewish laws and rituals. Unlike Christians, Jews do not believe Jesus is the Messiah. Instead, they have faith that the Messiah has yet to come.

How They Got Here

How did this religious mosaic come to be?

It is thought that two brothers who became Christian saints, Methodius and Cyril, were instrumental in converting tribal Slavs in the 800s. To help gain converts, they translated the Bible into a regional Slavic language. Saint Cyril even developed a new alphabet named after him, Cyrillic, based on Greek letters. It is still used today in much of Bosnia.

After the Great Schism of 1054, the Slovenes and Croats living in the northern reaches of the region tended to stay Catholic. The Serbs, who resided mainly in the southern and eastern lands of the area, became Eastern Orthodox. In 1346, Serbian emperor Stefan Dušan (1308–1355) founded a Serbian Orthodox Church patriarchate, or territory, officially ruled by a Serbian Orthodox patriarch whose power equalled that of a bishop. The Serbian Orthodox Church became a major religion in the southeast Balkans.

Stuck in the middle was Bosnia, which was home to followers of both the Roman Catholic and Eastern Orthodox Churches. In addition, as discussed in chapter one, a third branch of Christianity called Bogomilism had developed in the region. Under pressure, Bogomils left their faith in the 12th and 13th centuries. Some became Catholics while others started their own Bosnian Church.

It was after the Muslim Ottomans captured Constantinople, the capital of the Eastern Orthodox Church, in 1453 that the winds of change began blowing into southeastern Europe. Members of the Bosnian Church, including former Bogomils who were still feeling the ill effects of the crusade against their ancestors nearly 250 years earlier, willingly converted from Christianity to Islam. Most historians believe they are the direct ancestors of today's Bosniaks.

In 1492, less than a decade after the Ottoman capture of Constantinople, Jews were expelled from Spain and scattered throughout Europe. Many found tolerance in the city of Vrhbosna, later Sarajevo. Unlike Jews who lived in the Kingdom of Venice or many other parts of Europe, the Jews of Sarajevo were not forced to live in their own ghetto, separate from the rest of the city, and as a result their religion, culture, and language entered Bosnia.

SEEING THE HOLY PLACES

In a place as diverse and ancient as Bosnia and Herzegovina it is only natural that one will find some of the most intriguing religious sites in Europe. Ancient cathedrals, mosques, synagogues, and holy cemeteries abound in all parts of the nation, but if one had to narrow it down, the following four sites, relating to each of the four major creeds, would top anyone's list of the most significant religious places to see.

GAZI HUSREV-BEG'S MOSQUE

One of the most important and biggest mosques in the Balkans is the Gazi Husrev-beg's Mosque, known among Sarajevo residents as simply the Beg's Mosque. Gazi Husrev-beg was a governor of a Bosnian *sanjak,* or province, from 1521 to 1541. The mosque, with its sky-piercing minaret, or tower, from which calls to worship are chanted, was built around 1530. Its half dome ceiling rises 65 feet, making the interior airy and spacious. Gazi Husrev-beg and his freed slave are buried in a grave-yard in the rear of the mosque, while in a courtyard in front is a refresh-ing *shadrvan,* or water fountain, built in Byzantine style. The *shadrvan,* built just over 100 years ago, looks older than it is. The mosque was damaged during the Bosnian War and is being repaired.

ST. JAMES CHURCH

While there are numerous historic Catholic churches and other shrines in Bosnia and Herzegovina, what is likely the most visited Catholic site is rel-atively new. In fact, this site proves that religious history continues to be made in present times. On June 24, 1981, six teenagers reported that the image of Jesus' mother, the Virgin Mary, appeared to them in a mountain village called Medjugorje, located in Herzegovina not far from the Croat-ian border. Immediately, devout Catholics made pilgrimages to this poverty-stricken hamlet, turning it almost overnight into a tourist magnet.

The Catholic Church never officially verified the sightings, but that has not stopped followers from coming to Apparition Hill, the place

For most of the last 400 years, Bosnians identified themselves by their religion. But as nationalism came to the forefront under Austro-Hungarian rule in the latter 19th century, more and more Bosnians came to think of themselves as Bosniaks, Croats, or Serbs as

where the Virgin Mary supposedly appeared, which is now comme-
morated with a blue cross. Medjugorje's Catholic church, St. James
Church, built in 1969, has become a kind of headquarters for religious
pilgrims, and Cross Mountain, where a white cross was erected in 1934
in memory of the 1,900th anniversary of Jesus' death, is a popular des-
tination for visitors.

CHURCH OF ST. MICHAEL THE ARCHANGEL
Residents of Sarajevo know it simply as the Old Orthodox Church, but
the squatty gray-toned building is officially the Church of St. Michael
the Archangel. Its foundation dates back to either the fifth or sixth centuries while the actual structure is believed to have been constructed in
1539. The fairly plain exterior of St. Michael the Archangel belies the
lavish interior. There is an elaborately carved wooden screen used for
holding religious icons and a large balcony where women would be
seated.

SEPHARDIC JEWISH CEMETERY
Sarajevo is also home to one of the region's oldest synagogues, but
the most inspiring Jewish site might be the Sephardic Jewish cemetery
with tombstones inscribed in the 1500s. (The word *Sephardic* refers to
descendants of Jews from Spain or Portugal, as opposed to Russia or
other parts of northeastern Europe.) The inscriptions on the tombstones are in Ladino, an archaic language which combines medieval
Spanish and Hebrew, and is used almost exclusively by Jews in the
Balkans.

Included on the tombstones are symbolic patterns and motifs
peculiar to Sephardic Jewry. The cemetery was badly damaged during
the Bosnian War and is currently undergoing renovation and repair. In
the spring of 2001 the first phase of its preservation was completed.
Nearby is an old synagogue with a collection of rare Ladino books dating to the 1700s, and a museum detailing the history of Sarajevo's Jewish population.

---

well as Muslim, Catholic, or Eastern Orthodox. Under the communist
regime of Marshal Tito, religious worship was discouraged, and
Yugoslav as a cultural identity was encouraged. Large numbers of people referred to themselves as Yugoslavs.

Religion Today

Mosques, churches, and synagogues were destroyed as a part of ethnic cleansing during the Bosnian War. Today, these houses of worship are being quickly rebuilt. Both the destruction and the rebuilding of the religious shrines has little to do with religion, however, and much to do with ethnic pride. The people of Bosnia and Herzegovina, generally speaking, lean toward secularism. One removes one's shoes to enter a Muslim home, out of respect for Bosniak ethnicity as much as the Muslim religion.

Still, over the last several years religious practice has increased somewhat. This has been true mainly among younger Bosnians, especially Catholic Croats in the Herzegovina region of the nation.

The two political districts in Bosnia and Herzegovina are by their very nature almost entirely segregated by religion. Muslims and Catholics live mainly in the Federation, while Eastern Orthodox reside almost entirely in the Republika Srpska. The exceptions are the

The Sephardic Jewish cemetery in Sarajevo has tombstones dating to the 1500s. Damaged in the war, the old cemetery underwent its first phase of restoration in the spring of 2001. (Courtesy Free Library of Philadelphia)

Jews who mostly live in Sarajevo. Many live also in the communities of Banja Luka and Doboj in the RS and Mostar, Tuzla, and Zenica in the Federation.

THE POPE VISITS SARAJEVO

On the weekend of April 12 and 13, 1997, Pope John Paul II, leader of the Roman Catholic Church, made a visit to Sarajevo. He had originally planned to visit in September 1994, but Bosnian Serbs were in the midst of their siege of the city and warned that they could not guarantee the pope's safety. Since most Catholics live outside Sarajevo, the pope's 1997 visit was viewed as a test of freedom in Bosnia and Herzegovina. And with the attacks on Muslims and Catholics just two months earlier, there was tension in the air. Police conducted house to house searches along the pope's motorcade route from the airport into the city.

The pope spoke several times to different audiences, including many political leaders and representatives of the Jewish and Muslim communities of Sarajevo. He also conducted a public mass in Sarajevo. Although police discovered explosive devices along the motorcade route from the airport to the city center, and some Bosnian Serbs threatened to block access to Sarajevo across the RS, there were no major incidents. Some 45,000 Croat Catholics journeyed to Sarajevo for this once in a lifetime visit.

The Pope stressed that peace in Bosnia and Herzegovina was achievable, but depended on an act some considered hard to give: forgiveness. The elderly Pope pleaded:

Building a true and lasting peace is a great task entrusted to everyone. Certainly, much depends on those who have public responsibilities. But the future of peace, while largely entrusted to institutional formulations, which have to be effectively drawn up by means of sincere dialogue and in respect for justice, depend no less decisively on a renewed solidarity of minds and hearts. It is this interior attitude which must be fostered, both within the frontiers of Bosnia-Herzegovina and also in relations with neighboring States and the Community of Nations. But an attitude of this kind can only be established on the foundation of forgiveness. For the edifice of peace to be solid, against the background of so much blood and hatred, it will have to be built on the courage of forgiveness. People must know how to ask for forgiveness and to forgive!

To be certain that all religions, even minorities, would be welcome in Bosnia and Herzegovina, a clause was put into the country's constitution at the meeting of the Dayton Peace Agreement in 1995. It reads, "No person shall be deprived of Bosnia and Herzegovina or Entity citizenship on any ground such as sex, race, color, language, religion, political or other opinion, national or social origin, association with a national minority, property, birth or other status."

Still, there have been incidents of harassment and threats against members of nearly all religions. The government of the Federation mostly abided by the constitutional provision for freedom of religion. But within a few years after the Dayton Accords were signed, authorities of the RS government were caught trying to prevent returning refugees from visiting religious shrines and cemeteries in areas that had been their homes before the war. In one violent instance in the Federation in February 1997, Muslims at a West Mostar cemetery were shot at by Catholic Bosnian-Croatian police. In response, Muslims bombed and vandalized a number of Roman Catholic churches.

Acts of Intolerance

According to the 2001 Annual Report on International Religious Freedom, published by the Office of International Religious Freedom (OIRF) in the United States, respect for religious freedom in Bosnia and Herzegovina did not decline, and if anything may have gotten greater. More and more refugees were returning to areas in which theirs was the minority religion. More residents felt comfortable that their beliefs would be respected.

On the other hand, some returning refugees met resistance from nationalist local residents. Violent reactions were reported. For example, in May 2001, there were riots in the RS city of Trebinje when Muslims, trying to rebuild one of the 618 mosques destroyed during the Bosnian War, were attacked by about 1,500 Serb nationalists. The RS police did little to stop the violence. The next day a grenade was thrown at the house of the leader of the local Islamic community. Finally, after a few days, the police chief of Trebinje was fired, and several people involved in the harassment were arrested.

However, the punishments of the guilty were considered "extremely light," and while the RS government officially expressed regret about the riots, it also stated that "the reconstruction of religious buildings is being used for political purposes and is 'causing tension' in the RS."

A similar riot took place on May 7, 2001, at a rebuilding ceremony in the RS capital Banja Luka. While some RS police officers were dismissed for lack of action, the local government released a statement blaming the local Muslim community for stirring up passions by trying to rebuild mosques.

Some Bosniaks in the Federation responded to the Serb violence by attacking Serb Orthodox churches in areas where Islam is the majority religion. On May 8, 2001, Bosniaks threw a hand grenade at a Serb Orthodox church and smashed the windows of a Serb-owned café. Over the next few days a Serb-owned house was pummeled with stone and an Orthodox cemetery was desecrated.

There were instances of nonviolent discrimination, too. On June 4, 2001, the mayor of the Croat Catholic town of Stolac refused to permit local Muslims to rebuild a mosque that once stood in the town center. He insisted that a Catholic church, which had stood on the same spot before the mosque was constructed, should be rebuilt instead. Meanwhile, in the RS community of Pećnik, regional Catholic officials reported that Serb authorities in the town had been trying to demolish a Catholic church in the process of being rebuilt with the argument that the workers had no building permit.

The OIRF summed up, "Religious intolerance in the country directly reflects ethnic intolerance because the identification of ethnicity with religious background is so close as to be virtually indistinguishable."

Acts of Tolerance

On the other hand, there were also many improvements in religious tolerance in Bosnia and Herzegovina. In 2001, a total of five mosques in the Republika Srpska that had been destroyed in the war were rebuilt. In the town of Gradina, which has a Muslim majority, the local Islamic authority volunteered to remove a mosque constructed during the war since some of it is on Serb-owned land. In 2001, the RS national assembly ended its practice of opening its sessions with a Serbian Orthodox prayer. In addition, new assembly members no longer have to recite an Orthodox oath, but may choose an oath consistent with his or her own religion, or even a nonreligious oath if they wish. And on April 24, 2001, with Muslim and Croat members of the state assembly in attendance, the Mostar Jewish community laid a foundation stone for a new synagogue, which will be part of a larger Jewish community cultural center.

Prominent members of the various religious communities have openly expressed a desire to work together to end religious bigotry. Leaders of the Muslim, Catholic, Orthodox, and Jewish communities have formed the Interreligious Affairs Council of Bosnia and Herzegovina, which works closely with a U.S.-based private organization called the World Conference on Religion and Peace, in order to promote religious harmony in this corner of the globe. Another interfaith group working toward the same goals is the Organization for Security and Cooperation in Europe.

One of the biggest examples of religious brotherhood took place on June 8, 2001. A Catholic group called Sant'Egidio, whose purpose is to resolve conflicts, held a conference in Rome on religious reconciliation in Bosnia and Herzegovina. Muslim, Catholic, Orthodox, and Jewish people all sent representatives to the meeting. It resulted in a joint statement supporting the rebuilding of all religious sites in Bosnia and Herzegovina.

NOTES

p. 80 "The people of Bosnia and Herzegovina . . ." "Bosnia-Herzegovina: Background Info." Available on-line. URL: http://dest.travelocity.com/DestGuides. Downloaded November 20, 2001.

p. 81 "Some 45,000 Croat Catholics . . ." Defense Language Institute, Foreign Language Center (DLIFIC), of United States Defense Department, "World Religions and Cultures: The Linguists' Network," "Area Studies/South Central Europe: Bosnia Herzegovina." Available on-line. URL: http://wrc.lingnet.org/bosnia.htm. Downloaded September 17, 2002.

p. 81 " 'Building a true and lasting peace . . .' " "John Paul II Apostolic Visit to Sarajevo," 1997, "Address of the Holy Father to the Political Leaders of Bosnia-Herzegovina." Available on-line. URL: http://members.aol.com/rimac/bosfra/speeches.html. Downloaded September 19, 2002.

p. 82 " 'No person shall be deprived . . .' " "Constitution of Bosnia Herzegovina," United States Department of State Foreign Affairs Network (DOSFAN), November 21, 1995. Available on-line. URL: gopher://dosfan.lib.uic.edu/00ftp:DOSFan:Gopher:04%20Geographic%20Bureaus:05%Eu . . . . Downloaded September 20, 2002.

p. 82 "According to the 2001 Annual Report . . ." "International Religious Freedom Report Released by the Bureau of Democracy, Human Rights, and Labor," released October 26, 2001. Available on-line. URL: http://www.state.gov/g/drl/rls/irf/2001/5570pf.htm. Downloaded September 16, 2002.

p. 83 "'the reconstruction of religious buildings . . .'" "International Religious Freedom Report Released by the Bureau of Democracy, Human Rights, and Labor." Downloaded September 16, 2002.

p. 83 "'Religious intolerance . . .'" "International Religious Freedom Report Released by the Bureau of Democracy, Human Rights, and Labor." Downloaded September 16, 2002.

6

ECONOMY

For almost four years, the top priorities of most people living in Bosnia and Herzegovina was safety. After the war their basic needs were just a little more basic than those of people living anywhere. They needed clothes to keep them warm, roofs over their heads to stay safe from the elements, and food to keep them alive. They needed jobs to earn money, and prices had to be reasonable so that necessary products were affordable. Nothing has been easy in that regard.

All the former Soviet Union satellite states in Eastern Europe have faced a difficult task converting from a communist to a free-market economic system. Bosnia and Herzegovina has had to deal with that as well as recovering from an expensive and destructive war.

Following the fall of Tito's socialistic system in the early 1990s and before the war, Bosnia and Herzegovina and Macedonia were the poorest former Yugoslav republics. While Tito allowed private land ownership, most farms were very small and poorly run and, and Bosnia has traditionally been a net importer of food. And factories, which had been run by the federal government, were grossly mismanaged. A large number of these plants were involved in the business of metallurgy, specifically the processing of raw metals such as bauxite and aluminum. Many had extra workers on their staffs who were not needed; with a lot of people getting paid for doing very little work, profits were low.

Civil War

Then came the devastating war. Inflation ran rampant, reflecting the high cost of supporting the war. The Yugoslav government could not keep up with the demand for money, and at one point paper money denominations of up to 10 billion dinara were issued.

To complicate matters even more, the Bosnian Serbs issued their own currency, the Bosnian Serb dinar, which they printed in Banja Luka. The Croats and Muslims quickly followed suit. But the value of all three currencies kept dropping dramatically thanks to high inflation rates. In the fall of 1994, when the war seemed far from over, the nation of Yugoslavia released a new paper currency called the new dinar. One new dinar was equal to 10,000 old dinars. But with ever increasing inflation, few residents of any part of Yugoslavia trusted the paper money. It became virtually worthless.

Under normal circumstances, the government might have issued coin money instead of paper to halt inflation. However, metal was scarce during the war and its value was soon greater than what the face value of the coins would have been. Since people needed money with true value to make purchases, Yugoslavia decided to adopt a more stable currency, the German mark. At times they also used the U.S. dollar.

As a result of the four years of fighting, production in Bosnia and Herzegovina declined a whopping 80 percent. Its annual per capita income dropped from $1,900 in 1990 to $500 by the war's end. In the energy field alone, roughly 70 percent of electrical generating capacity was damaged due to transmission lines ruined during the war. Coal production dropped to less than 10 percent of its prewar level. In agriculture, devastation to farm equipment, livestock, and arable land during the war resulted in food production serving only 35 percent of the people's needs.

Foreign Aid

To try to help get the citizens of Bosnia and Herzegovina back on their feet, many nations, including the United States, have provided millions of dollars in aid. A U.S. government agency called the United

States Agency for International Development (USAID) oversees the program.

The organization's roots go back to the years immediately following World War II. The Marshall Plan, named after former secretary of state George Marshall, provided aid to reconstruct ravaged Europe. In 1961, President John F. Kennedy signed into law the Foreign Assistance Act, which created USAID. The purpose of such aid is to foster democracy and stability in other parts of the world, to establish good relations between other nations and the United States, and to improve the lives of impoverished people in the developing world.

In USAID's own words, its main purpose is "Establishing a policy and institutional framework conducive to the emergence of a market economy, by restoring private sector productive capacity and creating self-sustaining employment."

By August of 2000, the U.S. government had already given nearly $900 million to the government of Bosnia and Herzegovina. The total of worldwide foreign aid from the end of the war in 1996 through 2001 has been estimated at $5 billion.

The results have been mixed. The economy has been improving, but slowly. The change from Titoism to a free market economy has proven a considerable challenge. Obstacles have ranged from corrupt management to resistance to change. Some critics say that Bosnians, who before the war relied on the government to run their businesses, now expect the countries of the world to feed and shelter them. Joe Ingram, the World Bank's representative in Bosnia, states, "People feel that governments have to provide everything. There is that entitlement mentality which has to be broken."

Privatization has been mandated by laws passed in both the Federation and the RS. By July 2000 more than 200 socially owned businesses, 1,000 business premises, and socially owned assets were sold through small-scale privatization. The sales brought in more than 200 million dollars.

It was estimated that three-quarters of the Bosnian workforce was out of work in the year following the signing of the Dayton peace accords. Many more people are working today, but the official unemployment rate continues to be very high, at about 40 percent.

The Gray Economy

However, Joe Ingram of the World Bank reports that Bosnia's economic situation may not be as dour in reality as is reported. While he admits that Bosnia's statistical bureaus report the unemployment rate is 40 percent, Ingram relates that the real unemployment rate may be as low as 25 percent. He attributes the difference to what he refers to as the shadow economy, also known more informally as the gray economy, which exists because some operating businesses are not registered with the government. This is their way of avoiding having to pay high taxes or comply with numerous regulations, which some Bosnians consider excessive.

Ingram opines that there are pluses and minuses to the gray economy. On the one hand, it increases competition with "legitimate" businesses, causing all to work harder. On the other hand, it erodes the government's tax base, and so reduces the amount of dollars used for public services including education and health care. According to Ingram, the gray economy situation has reached the point where the negatives are outweighing the positives. The government's attempts to protect and educate the Bosnian people are being thwarted.

Two Entities or One

The two entities in Bosnia and Herzegovina are reporting opposite economic results. The economy in the Federation is generally performing better than that of the RS, the poorer district of a poor country, and the gap between the two entities is widening. The World Bank insists that the RS is dragging down the economic performance of the country as a whole, and recommends the two economies be integrated into a national one. The end result, says the World Bank, would be a much bigger market and greater opportunities.

That goal does not sit well with Bosnian nationalists, especially the Serbs, even though the RS is suffering. Leaders of the Bosnian Serb party, SDS, claim that integration into a single economic market would spark a weakening in Bosnian Serb cultural identity. As long as nationalists are in power, the dream of a single Bosnian economy is just that—a dream.

Cars, Steel, Machines, and Grain

About 19 percent of Bosnia and Herzegovina's gross domestic product comes from agriculture. About 23 percent is based on manufactured items, and 58 percent is made from providing services.

When it was part of Yugoslavia under Tito's leadership, Bosnia and Herzegovina was the arms-making capital of the country. Because of its mountainous location, Tito felt it was a secure place for weapons factories. Today, thanks mainly to the region's many mines, industry consists of metallurgy and primary metal processing, including steel.

Natural resources include iron ore, copper, lead, zinc, bauxite, and cobalt. Other basic products made here include textiles and timber products. Appliances and finished products manufactured in Bosnia include tool machines, tractors, optical instruments, bicycles, and television and radio receivers. Those who work the land in Bosnia have traditionally raised corn, wheat, oats, and barley, while farmers in the warmer climes of Herzegovina grow tobacco, cotton, and grapes.

Other countries have found that one helpful way to aid Bosnia and Herzegovina's people to economic recovery is not to simply give them aid but to invest in Bosnia's workers by locating branches of their businesses there. One of the biggest such companies is the German auto maker Volkswagen.

Before the war, Volkswagen manufactured Beetles, Golfs, and Jettas in a factory in Vogošća outside Sarajevo, but it was one of the many buildings destroyed during battles there. So in 1998 Volkswagen built and opened a new factory in Sarajevo. For four years it produced only Skoda models, which are sold in Europe and Asia, particularly in Bosnia, Croatia, and Turkey. Then in 2002 Volkswagen announced Volkswagen Sarajevo would begin assembling Golfs again. Volkswagen owns 58 percent of the business and a private company based in Bosnia owns the remaining 42 percent.

Another Bosnia and Herzegovina business operating with foreign help is a steel firm with a long history in the region. In 1892 an iron and steel mill owned by a company named Željezara Zenica opened in the Bosnian city of Zenica. During the Tito years it was like all businesses owned by the government. Then it suspended operations during the war in the early 1990s. But in 1998, an enterprise in the oil-rich Arabian nation of Kuwait, Kuwait Consulting & Investment Co., invested 60 million dollars to help the steelworks get back on its feet. With the merging of the two concerns, the business was given a new name: BH Steel Company.

THE POTATO CHIP MAN TO THE RESCUE

In spite of ethnic tensions and the enormous economic disadvantages here, there have been promising business start-ups among the people of Bosnia and Herzegovina. An internationally known humanitarian organization called CARE (Cooperative for Assistance for Relief Everywhere, Inc.) recently helped a Bosnian businessman named Ferid Mujanović establish a potato chip–making factory in Bosnia and Herzegovina. Mujanović has hired Muslims, Serbs, and Croats—basically, any hardworking person he could find—to work in his factory. Managers from CARE assisted Mujanović in acquiring the money he needed to start his business.

Adrian Green, CARE Project Manager, said of Mujanović,

He knew that everywhere he went, he could only eat potato chips imported from Germany, France, Italy, England, America. There's no earthly reason for that, because potatoes can be grown in Bosnia-Herzegovina. And he had this great idea. . . .

There are only two things people care about when you get right down to it in Bosnia-Herzegovina, because they are just the same as people everywhere else. They want jobs and they want stability for their family. Really, nothing else matters.

After two years of hard work, Mujanović's potato chip factory was up and running. Today it is thriving and Bosnians of all ethnicities are working side by side to make it happen.

Other foreign businesses with offices or factories in Bosnia and Herzegovina include a German cement company, Cementara Kakanj; an Austrian bank, Volksbank; and a Netherlands-based division of the U.S. soft drink company Coca-Cola.

But not everything is rosy for foreign investors. Because of ethnic political disputes, the Coca-Cola plant in Sarajevo has had trouble distributing their sodas in the RS to the point where it is easier to export their products to a separate country. In addition, bombed-out buildings are hardly welcoming to potential foreign investors.

Because not much of the mountainous nation has arable land, foodstuffs are among the country's biggest imports. Bosnia's countryside is filled with forests, making lumber products, including beech and pine in addition to veneer and construction lumber the mainstay of its exports. About half of its exports are raw products including minerals, charcoal, tobacco, and fruit. Some of the common finished products Bosnia and Herzegovina exports include furniture (especially chairs), jackets, pants, and knitwear made from cotton. However, it also sends to other nations everything from shoes to auto parts.

The New Currency

It is hoped that in time Bosnia and Herzegovina's volatile economy will settle down. Negotiators at the Dayton peace talks took steps in that direction when they defined the main goals and duties of the Central Bank. Less than two years after the peace agreement was signed, the Central Bank of Bosnia and Herzegovina was established by the national parliament on June 20, 1997. On August 11 that year, it began operation.

Then on June 22, 1998, the first banknotes were issued for the nation's newly devised currency, the convertible mark, or KM. A convertible mark consists of 100 pfenings, just as a dollar is made up of 100 pennies. The first bank notes were in the values of 50 pfenings and 1, 5, and 10 convertible marks. Then on December 9, 1998, Bosnia and Herzegovina's first coins in their new economic system were released in the value of 10, 20, and 50 pfenings. A year and a half later, on July 31, 2000, coins valued at 1 and 2 convertible marks were released.

Yet, nothing in this country comes easy. Not surprisingly, the Serbs, Muslims, and Croats disagreed intensely about what words and images should appear on the new money. Politicians could be put on the money without either the Serbs or the Muslims and Croats accusing the other side of playing favorites. At one point, the Serbs even threatened to issue their own currency, even though it would be in direct violation of the Dayton Peace Agreement.

A compromise was reached. Images of Bosnian writers would grace the fronts of the bills, and artistic and architectural images would appear on the backs. As a compromise within the compromise, both the Federation and the RS issued separate currencies. The Federation's paper money features Muslim and Croat authors, and the RS's bills show Serb writers. But all bills have the same color and design and all have the Central Bank of Bosnia and Herzegovina's name on it. One interesting side note is that

Bosnia and Herzegovina is the first nation to show only literary notables on their money.

The inscriptions on all the bills are written in both alphabets used in Bosnia and Herzegovina, Cyrillic—used mainly by Serbs—and Latin—practiced by Croats and Bosniaks. The bills were printed by a business in France and after they were placed in circulation, it became clear that the French company made serious errors with the Cyrillic characters. Some Serbs claimed that the printed mistakes were done purposely as a means of discrimination against them. However, most objective observers believe they were honest mistakes committed by French printers not familiar with the Cyrillic alphabet.

The Central Bank's main purpose is to maintain economic stability in the nation by releasing currency based on established agreements, and control the carrying out of Bosnia and Herzegovina's fiscal policies. The bank is led by a governing board and, like the political offices here, the membership of the board is comprised of political members. The head is a governor, or chairman, who is selected by the International Monetary Fund. Under him or her are three members, two from the Federation and one from the RS. The bank is headquartered in Sarajevo with subunits also in Sarajevo as well as Banja Luka and Mostar. Two smaller branches are in Pale and Brčko District.

NOTES

p. 86 "Following the fall of Tito's socialist system . . ." European Forum, "The Economic Situation of Bosnia and Hercegovina." Available on-line. URL: http://www.europeanforum.bot-consult.se/cup/bosnia/econ.htm. Downloaded November 19, 2001.

p. 87 "As a result of the four years of fighting . . ." European Forum, "The Economic Situation of Bosnia and Hercegovina."

p. 87 "Its annual per capita income . . ." The World Bank Group, "Reconstruction of Bosnia and Herzegovina: Priorities for Recovery and Growth." Available on-line. URL: http://www.worldbank.org/html/extdr/extme/bhgen.html. Downloaded September 24, 2002.

p. 87 "In the energy field alone . . ." The World Bank Group, "Reconstruction of Bosnia and Herzegovina: Energy." Available on-line. URL: http://www.worldbank.org/html/extdr/extme/energy.html. Downloaded September 24, 2002.

p. 87 "Coal production dropped . . ." The World Bank Group, "Reconstruction of Bosnia and Herzegovina: Energy."

p. 87 "In agriculture, devastation . . ." The World Bank Group, "Reconstruction of Bosnia and Herzegovina: Agriculture." Available on-line. URL: http://www.worldbank.org/html/extdr/agric.html. Downloaded September 24, 2002.

p. 88 "'Establishing a policy . . .'" The United States Agency for International Development, "Country Profile: Bosnia-Herzegovina." Available on-line. URL: http://www.usaid.gov/countries/ba/bos.htm. Downloaded November 20, 2001.

p. 88 "By August of 2000 . . ." The United States Agency for International Development. "Country Profile: Bosnia-Herzegovina."

p. 88 "'People feel that . . .'" Personal correspondence from Naomi Halewood, Development Data Group, World Bank, received April 30, 2003.

p. 88 "Privatization has been mandated . . ." Martin Sergeant, "Invest in Bosnia?" BBC News World Edition, July 3, 2002. Available on-line. URL: http://news.bbc.co.uk/2/hi/business/2088600.stm. Downloaded January 9, 2003.

p. 88 "It was estimated that . . ." The United States Agency for International Development, "Bosnia and Herzegovina: Regional Overview." Available on-line. URL: http://www.usaid.gov/country/ee/ba/. Text taken from the FY 2003 Congressional Budget Justification. Downloaded September 24, 2002.

p. 89 "While he admits that . . ." The United States Agency for International Development, "Country Profile: Bosnia-Herzegovina."

p. 89 "Ingram opines that there are . . ." Joe Ingram, "Bosnia's Shadow Economy." Available on-line. URL: http://www.worldbank.org.ba/ECA/Bosnia&Herzegovina.nsf/0/A1CADDE1841F1CE9C1256BDF004F7D69?Opendocument. Downloaded January 9, 2003.

p. 90 "About 19 percent . . ." Joe Ingram, "Bosnia's Shadow Economy."

p. 90 "Before the war, Volkswagen manufactured . . ." "Bosnia and Herzegovina." Available on-line. URL: http://www.cia.gov/cia/publications/factbook/geos/bk.html. Downloaded January 10, 2003.

p. 90 "But in 1998, an enterprise . . ." Reuters News Service, "VW JV in Bosnia Starts Assembling Golfs," July 3, 2002. Available on-line. URL: http://www.wardsauto.com/ar/transportation_vw_vowdge_jv/index.htm. Downloaded September 23, 2002.

p. 91 "Because of ethnic political disputes . . ." Steel Times, "1999 Annual Technical Review of European Steel Making." Available on-line. URL: http://www.dmg.co.uk/steeltimes/review/bosnia.htm. Downloaded September 23, 2002.

p. 91 "'He knew that everywhere he went . . .'" Martin Sergeant, "Invest in Bosnia?" Download January 9, 2003.

p. 91 "'There are only . . .'" Gretchen Hemes, "Bosnia-Herzegovina: Potato Chips for Peace and Prosperity," January 14, 2001. Available on-line. URL: http://www.careusa.org/newsroom/featurestories/2002/jan/01042001_bosnia.asp.

p. 91 "But not everything is rosy . . ." Martin Sargeant, "Invest in Bosnia?"

7

CULTURE

Thanks to the presence of Muslims, Serbs, Croats, and Sephardic Jews, this unusual nation has developed a culture influenced by a wide variety of different people. The fact that there is no one indigenous ethnic populace has exposed Bosnia and Herzegovina to a truly broad spectrum of music, literature, theater, and other arts.

Language

The language of most of the people of Bosnia and Herzegovina—as well as most of what was Yugoslavia—is Serbo-Croatian. It is spoken by about 20 million people across the world, including between 100,000 and 200,000 in North America, and has three distinct dialects. The one spoken mostly in Bosnia and Herzegovina is called Ijekavian, which includes many words borrowed from the languages of western Europe.

Serbo-Croatian has 25 consonants and five vowels. Most Bosnians speak Serbo-Croatian, but they have different ways of writing it. Bosnian Serbs use the Cyrillic alphabet, based on the Greek alphabet. Its creators, Saint Cyril and Saint Methodius, added letters to represent Slavic sounds not found in Greek. It contains 33 characters and five solid vowels.

Bosnian Croats and Muslims use the Latin (Roman) alphabet, also derived from the Greek alphabet, and the same one used in the English language.

Music

In a nation that straddles the borders of East and West, Bosnia and Herzegovina's traditional folk music has a definite eastern influence. After the Ottomans conquered the land in the 15th century, Islamic musical tendencies found their way into Bosnian songs. This was especially true in the cities, where Muslim religious practices were most common. The chants of Muslim mystics called the Sufis can be heard in the folk renderings of Bosniaks (Muslim Bosnians) and Sephardic Jews alike.

The influence of traditional Ottoman music was felt in the cities but did not affect people living in the rural areas of Bosnia. In the days long before electronic mass communications, the mountainous terrain kept the peoples of the villages isolated. Their folk music tends to reflect that of the Croats and Serbs.

Just as gospel church music has influenced African-American pop music, including rhythm and blues and Motown, the religious music of Bosnian Muslims can be heard in ancient Bosnian love songs. The most famous type of love song is the *sevdalinka*, a beautiful but mournful ballad of unreturned love. Since under strict Islamic practice men and women are segregated, music has provided the only excuse for them to be together. Many *sevdalinka*s include lyrics reflecting the desire for happier times, a common feeling among the people of Bosnia and Herzegovina in various times in their history and many aspects of their lives.

Traditional music here was not played on guitars or violins so common in the West. Bosnians have their own favorite stringed instruments, most notably the *tamburitza*, which according to local rural legend makes music so hauntingly lovely that even goats would dance to it.

The *tamburitza* consists of an egg-shaped gourd attached to a long neck. Some say it resembles a cross between a lute and a mandolin, and most music historians regard it as Bosnia and Herzegovina's national instrument. *Tamburitza*s may have two single strings to three courses of double strings, depending on the context in which they will be played. At

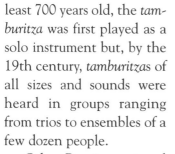

The gusle *is one of Bosnians' favorite folk instruments. Older Bosnians have taught it to younger generations for years.* (Courtesy United Nations)

least 700 years old, the *tamburitza* was first played as a solo instrument but, by the 19th century, *tamburitzas* of all sizes and sounds were heard in groups ranging from trios to ensembles of a few dozen people.

Other Bosnian stringed instruments handed down from one generation to the next include the *tambura, gusle, sargija,* and *saz,* all also similar to the lute. The *saz* resembles a traditional Greek mandolin called a *bouzouki* and was commonly used to accompany both western and eastern-style dancers and singers. Much of the time it was heard in musical breaks of *sevdalinkas.*

Perhaps the most popular nonstringed instrument in Bosnia is of Turkish origin, the *zurna.* It is a double-reeded music maker with a long wooden body flaring into a wide bell at its end. Among western instruments its sound most resembles the oboe's. Like the *tamburitza,* it can be played solo or in multiple numbers in a group, and in fact is associated with Turkish military marching bands. In addition, percussion instruments such as the *kudum,* or kettledrum, and *zil,* or cymbal, were played for years in Bosnian folk activities such as weddings or other family celebrations.

By the 1900s folk musicians could make good livings playing at *kafanas,* or cafes, in Sarajevo and the other cities of Bosnia and Herzegovina.

These professional singers and musicians were in many ways like folk balladeers, performing *sevdalinkas* or epic tunes telling the tales of events in the history and folklore of the Bosnian people.

Until the 1940s, professional performance was a man's job in Bosnia and Herzegovina. Because of strict Muslim social laws, women were for a long time discouraged from singing in public. They shared their musical talents behind closed doors in their immediate family circles, singing *sevdalinkas* as well as wedding and religious songs and lullabies.

Most recently Bosniaks, especially those in cities, have borrowed musical traditions from their Croatian, Serbian, and Jewish neighbors to add new touches to their centuries-old musical styles, including *sevdalinkas*. Western instruments including the accordion, bass guitar, and violin have, in the last few decades, jazzed up the basic Bosnian repertoire, and in doing so have given *sevdalinkas* a popularity they had not seen in a long time.

This is not to say that young Bosnians do not have their own music. Beginning in the mid-1960s, the raucous sounds of rock and roll could be heard wafting through club windows in cities in Bosnia and Herzegovina and the rest of the former Yugoslavia. One of the earliest home-grown Bosnian rock bands that became famous in the clubs of Sarajevo was Indeksi. They played a form of California surf music like the Beach Boys, although the lyrics were written and sung in their native language. Indeksi changed with the times. By the late 1960s they had a more psychedelic sound.

Perhaps Bosnia's most renowned band was Bijelo Dugme, translated in English as "white button." Fronted by guitarist Goran Bregović, Bijelo Dugme blasted its way to fame playing the stadiums and arenas of the Balkans. Bijelo Dugme were Bosnian masters of metal and one critic compared them to Led Zeppelin. Although Bijelo Dugme played live and recorded into the 1980s, punk and new wave music had captured the hearts and minds of Bosnia's young people in the late 1970s, just as it had elsewhere. The most powerful names in the Sarajevo punk scene included the bands Zabranjeno Pušenje (translated as "no smoking") and Elvis Kurtovič and His Meteors.

Sarajevo continued to be the center of the Bosnian rock world throughout the 1980s, although most of the critically lauded musicians were based in other parts of Yugoslavia. The Bosnian War deadened the region's rock scene and it has had a hard time rebuilding.

GORAN BREGOVIĆ

To rock music fans of Bosnia, he is Elvis Presley, John Lennon, Bob Dylan, and Paul Simon rolled into one. Goran Bregović was born in Sarajevo in 1950, the son of a Serbian mother and Croatian father. As a youngster, he studied violin before exchanging it for a guitar. He recalled, "I chose guitar because guitar players always have most success with girls."

He formed Bijelo Dugme as a teenager and discovered that his music did more than allow him to meet members of the opposite sex. It also allowed him to express aloud opinions that in a communist country could have been viewed as treasonous. Bregović admitted, "In those times rock had a capital role in our lives. It was the only way we could make our voice heard, and publicly express our discontent without risking jail (or just about . . ."

Bregović and his band lived the lives of rock superstars in Eastern Europe for over a decade and a half until he tired of the hard living scene in 1985. After 13 albums, Bregović decided to give Bijelo Dugme a permanent rest. During his time as a touring rocker, Bregović met bass player Emir Kusturica of the punk band Zabranjeno Pušenje ("no smoking"). When they met again in the late 1980s, Kusturica had given up music for movie directing. Bregović was then living a quiet life in his small dream house on the Adriatic Coast.

Kusturica convinced Bregović to try his hand at writing for movies. That was the beginning of a collaboration for the two Bosnian former rock superstars. Bregović wrote the score for Kusturica's film *Time of the Gypsies,* released in 1988, and the first of several projects Kusturica and Bregović have collaborated on together.

During the Bosnian War, Bregović left his home for the safety of Paris, France. But when the war was over, he went back to performing. In 1995, he organized a highly unusual concert. He put together a band of 10 members, a vocal ensemble of 50 singers, and a symphony, and they toured Greece, Sweden, and Belgium. In the late 1990s, he toured Europe with a considerably smaller group Goran Bregović and His Wedding and Funeral Band. When not busy with touring, he wrote musical scores for stage plays. Responding to the heartache of the Bosnian War, Bregović gathered together three singers of three different religions, hired a Serbian Orthodox choir from Belgrade, Yugoslavia, and located a Catholic string section from Poznań, Poland. They all joined his Wedding and Funeral Band for a concert in Rome titled, "Amen: A Concert of Reconciliation." The December concert was televised on Italian television in early 2001.

Art

All a visitor to Bosnia and Herzegovina has to do is take a walk through some of the ancient Bogomil cemeteries and he or she will learn that the people here have been artists for centuries. Carved figures of animals, dancing humans, and other designs deck these 900-year-old tombstones.

And while Islam traditionally forbids graphic representations of the human form, Bosnian Muslims have never shied away from that practice in their artistic expression. One can also see traditional Islamic artistic elements such as intricate metalwork and complex calligraphy in Bosnian art in museums, in the gates, wooden ceilings, and furniture in the private homes and public religious structures of Bosnia and Herzegovina.

Silk embroideries, elaborately handwoven carpets (called kilims), and knotted rugs are among the many examples of textile art that have existed here for ages. For centuries and until the last few decades a common wedding gift was a handmade dowry rug inscribed with the young couple's initials and wedding date.

As might be expected, the life, death, and other dramas of the Bosnian War have found their ways into the projects of the nation's modern

Every possible venue is utilized for screening purposes during the Sarajevo Film Festival. In this case, a high school yard was adapted for movie audiences during the 1996 festival. (Courtesy Paul Grivas, Sarajevo Film Festival)

day artists. Among the best known were three former graphic design and art students from Sarajevo who created pop art together under the appropriate name "Trio." (Pop art, made famous in the early 1960s by Andy Warhol and other young American artists, uses techniques of commercial art and illustration to depict aspects of everyday life.) Husband and wife Bojan and Dadila Hadžihalilović and a friend named Lela Hatt formed the original Trio. Hatt has since relocated to Switzerland, and has been replaced in Trio by a young artist named Šejla Kamerić.

Although Trio organized before the war, the tragedy of the early 1990s has since dominated their work. Even during the material shortages during the war Trio scrimped and saved anything that could be used as an artistic medium. An example was a poster of the Olympics logo of five joined rings made to appear like barbed wire. Dadila Hadžihalilović explained, "I think we're typical of this place—simple, openhearted, emotional, but with a lot of humor. Sarajevo humor tends to be directed inward and be a little black. We're trying to show the world our soul."

Film and Theater

Sarajevo's population grows by approximately 100,000 people annually for about nine days every August as film fans and artists attend the Sarajevo Film Festival. While it has taken place only since 1995, Sarajevo's tribute to the world's movie creators has grown into one of the most highly regarded such events.

Of course, the movies of Bosnian filmmakers, many from the Sarajevo Academies of Fine and Performing Arts, are screened here. But the event really belongs to the movie industry of the world. The program for the 2002 Sarajevo Film Festival read in part, "The films in this year's Panorama represent all the continents: Africa, Asia, Australia, Europe, North and South America. (Only Antarctica is missing, but we will check that out for next year.)" Two movies first screened at the festival, which later became hits in the United States, included *Crouching Tiger, Hidden Dragon* and *About a Boy*.

The festival also has a special children's program. During the 2002 fest, 3,000 children were bused in twice a day to see *Stuart Little 2*. Some of these children had never been to a movie in their lives.

But things have been tough for Bosnia's own camera artists. It costs a lot of money to make movies—something that Bosnia's filmmakers almost never have. It is common in Europe especially to receive funding from government agencies devoted to helping those in the arts complete their projects.

Meanwhile, Bosnia's infrastructure needs rebuilding, and former refugees need help settling again. That is where the Bosnian government has placed its primary focus. One Bosnian filmmaker, Nenad Dizdarević, conceded, "My country is destroyed. There are a lot of priorities. Film is not as important as a lot of other things." So Dizdarević moved to France and received financial help from the French government to produce his films.

Ex punk-rocker Emir Kusturica, formerly the bass player of the band Zabranjeno Pušenje, is regarded as the premier Bosnian movie maker today, but he is only one of many making names for themselves. In 1994, at age 39, promising filmmaker Nenad Dizdarević produced An Awkward Age the first feature film to come out of Bosnia since the breakup of Yugoslavia. The movie centers around the stories of a group of teenagers coming of age in Sarajevo in the 1920s. The setting might be a time long past, but Dizdarević masterfully tells the tales of their first loves, their rebellions, and their conflicts with one another in ways that teenagers of any generation can relate to.

Sarajevo native Ademir Kenović is another Bosnian filmmaker who has achieved worldwide acclaim. Born in 1950, Kenović has been making feature movies since 1986, but became best known for his 1996 release, The Perfect Circle. The Perfect Circle centers on the lives of three people during the war: an alcoholic poet in Sarajevo and two orphaned brothers, ages seven and nine, whom the poet cares for while Sarajevo is under siege. In time he becomes like a second father to the boys and the three struggle to survive the war.

Like Nenad Dizdarević and Emir Kusturica, Danis Tanović was also born in 1955. Tanović's first feature film, No Man's Land, was released in 2001 and earned several honors that year, including the Sarajevo Film Festival's award for best first feature, and best screenplay at the Cannes Film Festival. No Man's Land is what some might consider typically Bosnian in that it looks at the Bosnian War with an edgy and dark sense of humor. Tanović portrays United Nations Protection Force (UNPROFOR) staff members as idle buffoons, the media covering the war as overly aggressive, and the soldiers as former friendly neighbors who now must hate each other. Tanović explained, "Characters in this story look quite alike. They are simple people, almost antiheroes, caught in the jaws of war. A man on one side of the front line could easily be found on the other. Only his name would be different."

Probably the most widely discussed and screened movie about the Bosnian War, titled *Bosna!*, was not made by Bosnians. This very graphic documentary about the Bosnian War was the work of two Frenchmen, Bernard-Henri Lévy and Alain Ferrari.

The theme of war has also found its way onto the stage, in the musical *Romeo & Juliet in Sarajevo*. But like the movie *Bosna!*, this drama was not primarily the work of Bosnian artists. The mastermind behind setting Shakespeare's classic play of doomed romance in the streets of 1990s Sarajevo was Russian-Austrian composer Sergei Dreznin. Dreznin gave Bosnians major parts in the productions and much of the dialogue was provided by an esteemed author and editor named Miroslav Prstojević, from Trebinje in Bosnia and Herzegovina. Also, the actors who played Romeo and Juliet, Siniša Stork and Nataša Mirković, respectively, in the original cast production, are Bosnian natives.

In this version of the famous tragedy, Romeo is an Orthodox Serb and Juliet is a Bosniak, and like Shakespeare's lovers Romeo and Juliet, they die in each other's arms. Unlike Shakespeare's version, a waiter at the café where Romeo and Juliet met sells their story to a foreign reporter for $6,000, and the two become international symbols of the war.

Material for *Romeo & Juliet in Sarajevo* came not just from Shakespeare, but from a real event. A Serb named Boško Brkić and a Bosniak named Admira Ismić, both 25 years old, were in love, and in May 1993 while trying to cross Sarajevo's Vrbanja Bridge to safety, they were both shot. Boško died right away, and although wounded, Admira crawled to his side where she died. Their bodies lay in the street for a week until the Serbs buried them in a Serbian cemetery. After the war was over, Ismić's father had their bodies exhumed and reburied in the Lion's Cemetery in Sarajevo, the final resting place of thousands of other war victims.

Romeo & Juliet in Sarajevo premiered in 1995 in Vienna, Austria, then toured in both Croatia and Bosnia. It received wonderful reviews from theater critics throughout Europe.

EMIR KUSTURICA

Just after trading his bass guitar for a movie camera, Kusturica, only 26 years old, produced a coming-of-age story titled *Do You Remember Dolly Bell?* It was released in 1981 and earned him a prestigious Golden Lion award for best first film presented at the Venice Film Festival in Italy. It takes place in Sarajevo in the 1960s and tells the story of a young man who gets hooked into the world of small-time crooks. He is hired to hide a young prostitute from authorities and he gradually falls in love with her. Critics raved about its compelling story but also about its depiction of a personal side of life in Yugoslavia.

Close looks at private lives became a common theme for Kusturica's movies. His next film, *When Father Was Away on Business* (1985), presents life and politics in Sarajevo from the point of view of a six-year-old boy. It earned a Golden Palm award for best picture at the Cannes Film Festival and the equivalent of five Oscars in Yugoslavia. His worth on his subsequent film, *Time of the Gypsies,* won him the best director award at the Cannes Film Festival in France. It was his first collaboration with Goran Bregović.

Wanting to try something different in 1991, Kusturica made his first English-language film with English-speaking actors. *Arizona Dream* starred an unlikely mix of performers including Johnny Depp, Jerry Lewis, and Faye Dunaway. The movie is a comedy-drama with a bizarre plot about a man forced to attend a wedding against his will where he

Literature

Like Bosnia's movie makers, Bosnian writers are virtually unknown outside of Eastern Europe. The Bosnian writer whose name is most recognizable outside his nation is most likely Ivo Andrić.

Andrić aside, most Bosnians are very familiar with the poetry and stories of a Bosniak named Skender Kulenović, the epic poems of 19th- and early-20th-century Serb Filip Višnjić, the outspoken words of journalist/poet and Herzegovina native Mehmedalija Mak Dizdar, and prominent Bosniak author Meša Selimović, best known for his narrative novels of Bosnian history and self-reflection *Death and The Dervish: Writings from an Unbound Europe* and *The Fortress: Writings from an Unbound Europe.*

falls in love with both a mother and her daughter. In several scenes, Kusturica pays tribute to famous movie directors including Alfred Hitchcock, but the movie did poorly in the United States. According to some critics, was too offbeat for American audiences.

Kusturica went back to what he does best. In 1995, he made a typical Bosnian black comedy titled *Underground,* which was a hit. Set in the early 1940s, it tells the tale of a group of people who hide in a cellar to escape authorities and are not able to leave for nearly 20 years. *Underground* was meant to be a metaphor for the history of Kusturica's native land. In 1998, after a short retirement, Kusturica made a wild comedy called *Black Cat, White Cat,* which centered on a feud between two Roma families. In this film Kusturica pays tribute to many different directors, from Federico Fellini to Mack Sennett. *Black Cat, White Cat* was well received by both audiences and critics.

Kusturica's thoughts of retirement in the mid-1990s were premature. In 2001, he tried acting in another director's film. *The Widow of St. Pierre* is a kind of morality play made by French director Patrice Leconte. The setting is French Canada in 1850. In the story, a drunk fisherman, played by Kusturica, commits a murder and is sentenced to die by guillotine. But there is no guillotine in the town and the fisherman must wait for one to arrive from France. In the meantime he becomes an upstanding citizen, causing the townspeople to think twice about putting him to death.

It appears that the world has not heard the last of Emir Kusturica.

Selimović had planned on writing a third book in the series before his death in 1982.

Modern-day Bosniak writer Semezdin Mehmedinović made a name for himself with *Sarajevo Blues,* his tortured account of ethnic cleansing in action in the early 1990s. Born just one year before Ivo Andrić received a Nobel Prize, Mehmedinović represents a new generation and has been praised by critics for his expressions of raw emotion, from anger and torment to guilt for grieving after his elderly father's death while at the same time the constant death from the war in his backyard in Sarajevo "only filled him with a dull sense of dread."

Perhaps the most unlikely literary hero to come out of Bosnia recently was a pre-teen Sarajevo girl named Zlata Filipović who began keeping a diary in November 1991, when she was not quite 11 years old. The daughter of a lawyer and a chemist, Zlata came from a very comfortable home but she wrote about what many girls her age would write about: watching MTV, dancing at her friends' birthday parties, going to school, and looking forward to sleeping in on Saturday mornings. "LONG LIVE SATURDAYS!" she wrote in her diary on one Friday afternoon, September 27, 1991.

But in April 1992 her world turned upside down. War had reached Sarajevo. On April 5, she captured how her old carefree life was conflicting with her new perilous one, "I'm trying to concentrate so I can do my

IVO ANDRIĆ

When Ivo Andrić was born in 1892 in the village of Dolac, near the city of Travnik, his homeland was part of the Austro-Hungarian Empire. When he died in 1975, it was in its waning years under the benign dictatorship of Tito. He lived through many changes.

In 1945, Andrić set the literary world on fire when he published three long works including what became his best known book, *The Bridge on the Drina.* His tales of the multireligious and multiethnic life of Bosnia earned Andrić the 1961 Nobel Prize in literature.

When the craggy-faced Andrić, with his receding hairline and thick glasses, stood up to accept his honor, he said,

> My country is indeed a small country between the worlds, as it has aptly been characterized by one of our writers, . . . a country which, at break-neck speed and at the cost of great sacrifices and prodigious efforts, is trying in all fields, including the field of culture, to make up for those things of which it has been deprived by a singularly turbulent and hostile past. In choosing the recipient of this award you have cast a shining light upon the literary activity of that country, at the very moment when, thanks to a number of new names and original works, that country's literature is beginning to gain recognition through an honest endeavor to make its contribution to world literature.

Andrić had much reason to be grateful. At the beginning of World War I when he was a budding poet, Andrić was put in prison for taking part in what were considered anti-Austrian activities. Between the world wars he served as a Yugoslav diplomat to other European countries, but after Germany invaded Yugoslavia in 1941, he was forced to live in seclu-

homework (reading), but I simply can't. Something is going on in town. You can hear gunfire from the hills."

From then until she was airlifted to safety in Paris, France, in December 1993, her day to day writings were concerned less about school and MTV, and more about hiding in cellars and losing her best friend in a bomb attack. The diary of this perceptive girl—some call her the 1990s version of Anne Frank—was first published in Serbo-Croatian but has since been translated into more than 20 languages and released all over the world. Zlata and her family have donated income from the book to found a charity to help Bosnian War victims, especially children.

---

sion in the capital of Belgrade. It was during his years of hiding during the war that he wrote *Bosnian Story, The Woman from Sarajevo,* and *The Bridge on the Drina.* Each was published right after the war ended, and Andrić continued writing short stories and essays until his death.

The real Drina bridge is a beautiful structure built in the early 1500s under Ottoman rule. Andrić uses it as a metaphor in *The Bridge on the Drina* to symbolize the links between many diverse people living in Bosnia. In the book, he says:

> In all tales about personal, family or public events the words 'on the bridge' could always be heard. Indeed on the bridge over the Drina were the first steps of childhood and the first games of boyhood. . . .
>
> The Christian children, born on the left bank of the Drina, crossed the bridge at once in the first days of their lives, for they were always taken in their first week to be christened. But all the other children, those who were born on the right bank and the Muslim children who were not christened at all, passed, as had once their fathers and their grandfathers, the main part of their childhood on or around the bridge. They fished around it or hunted doves under its arches.

Since October 10, 1976, Andrić's Belgrade apartment has been open to the public as a museum. Diehard fans and casual tourists come to see everything from original manuscripts and the Nobel Prize to his study and salon, which are decorated to look as they did when he lived there.

While some Muslims have considered his writings anti-Muslim, Andrić still has his share of admirers. An American human rights advocacy group, Physicians for Human Rights, which shared a Nobel Peace Prize in 1997, has placed *The Bridge on the Drina* on its list of recommended reading for those interested in the situation in Bosnia.

NOTES

p. 95 "The language of most . . ." UCLA Language Materials Serbo-Croatian Language Profile, "Serbo-Croatian Profile." Available on-line. URL: http://www.lmp.ucla.edu/profiles/profs01.htm. Downloaded September 27, 2002.

p. 99 " 'I chose guitar because . . .' "Goran Bregović website, "Goran Bregović and His Wedding and Funeral Band." Available on-line. URL: http://www.goranbegovic.co.yu/foreign/bioeng.htm. Downloaded September 29, 2002.

p. 99 " 'In those times rock had . . .' " Goran Bregović website.

p. 101 " 'I think we're typical . . .' " Tyler Marshall, "Ironic Postcards from a City at War," *Los Angeles Times,* World Report, March 28, 1995. Available on-line. URL: http://www.cco.caltech.edu/~bosnia/culture/postcard.html. Downloaded September 26, 2002.

p. 101 " 'The films in this year's Panorama . . .' " Howard Feinstein, "Panorama 2002," August 16, 2002. Available on-line. URL: http://www.sff.ba/Program/P-Panorama.shtml. Downloaded September 26, 2002.

p. 101 "Some of these children had . . ." Joan Dupont, "A Film Industry Held Prisoner of War," *International Herald Tribune,* August 30, 2002. Available on-line. URL: http://www.iht.com/cgibin/generic.cgi?template+articleprint.tmplh&ArticleId+69126. Downloaded September 29, 2002.

p. 102 " 'My country is destroyed . . .' " Associated Press, "Balkan Directors' Dilemma: Compelling Subjects, Scarce Funds," *The Toronto Sun,* September 11, 1997. Available on-line. URL: http://www.canoe.ca/filmfestor/sep11_balkan.html. Downloaded September 29, 2002.

p. 103 " 'Characters in this story . . .' " Danis Tanović, "Director's Statement." Available on-line. URL: http://www.unitedartists.com/nomansland/images/director_text3.gif. Downloaded September 29, 2002.

p. 105 " 'only filled him with a dull sense of dread.' " Semezdin Mehmedinović. *Sarajevo Blues,* (San Francisco: City Lights Books, 1998), p. 2.

p. 106 " 'LONG LIVE SATURDAYS!' " Zlata Filipović, *Zlata's Diary* (New York: Viking Press, 1994), p. 2.

pp. 106–107 " 'I'm trying to concentrate . . .' " Filipović, p. 31.

p. 106 " 'My country is indeed . . .' " "Ivo Andrić—Acceptance Speech," Nobel E-Museum. Available on-line. URL: http://www.nobel.se/literature/laureates/1961/andric-acceptance.html. Downloaded September 26, 2002.

p. 107 " 'In all tales about . . .' " Ivo Andrić, *The Bridge on the Drina,* (Chicago: University of Chicago Press, 1984), p. 15.

8
Daily Life

One would not expect life to be easy in a nation that just 10 years earlier, suffered through a catastrophic war and is continuing to rebuild. But life does go on. People continue to go to work to earn their livelihoods. Children still go to school and celebrate birthdays. Families worship at their mosques, churches, and synagogues. And all enjoy their traditional foods at the kitchen table.

Housing

Most of the people in Bosnia and Herzegovina live outside cities. Before the war, only 18 percent lived in cities. Since the war has ended, a huge number of people have been displaced. The war took a disastrous toll on the country's buildings. It has been estimated that 63 percent of Bosnia and Herzegovina's housing units sustained some damage during those four violent years. Of those, about 18 percent were defined as destroyed, or suffering more than 60 percent damage.

Like city dwellers in many countries, a high number of Bosnia's urban residents live in apartments, most of them prefabricated. Sarajevo alone, a city of 374,000, has more than 145,000 apartments. A little more than half of those are privately owned, most of the rest—holdovers from the days of Tito and his unique form of socialized government—are owned by the government.

U.S. Army vehicle, part of IFOR, passes on regular patrol through the village of Saša Memići, about 30 miles east of Tuzla. These patrols are necessary to make certain that refugees feel sufficiently secure to return to their homes. (AP/Wide World Photos/Sasa Kralj)

The vast majority of people living in the countryside make their homes in single family houses. Of those, most are cozy by American standards, averaging about 600 square feet in total size. (An average seven room house in the United States can range from 1,500 to 2,000 square feet.) That small area is often carved up into six or more rooms, and it is not uncommon for two or three generations of a family to share one house.

Much of the media, especially in North America, has portrayed the people of Bosnia and Herzegovina as peasants living in extreme poverty. Certainly, the nation has large areas of true poverty. Many living in rural Bosnia do not have electricity or running water; therefore, they have no indoor bathrooms. However, most Bosnians do have such modern amenities. A substantial number have cars, television sets, videocassette recorders, and computers.

Education

Like most systems in postwar Bosnia and Herzegovina, education is still in flux. (See chapter 10.) But even while the country rebuilds its education system, by law young people still must attend school.

Bosnia's general public education structure has changed little since the days of Tito and is not much different than that of many other nations. Children attend primary (elementary) school for eight years. The mandatory starting age is seven, and children are required to stay in school until the age of 15. Similar to the American system, for the first four of those years they stay in a single classroom throughout the school day and one teacher instructs them in all subjects. Starting with the fifth year, students are taught separate subjects by teachers with specialties in each.

After completing eighth grade, students have the choice of dropping out, attending a vocational school to learn a trade, or attending what is called in many central European countries a gymnasium. The term *gymnasium* in this part of the world does not mean a place to play sports but a school where the emphasis is on academics rather than a trade. Students can receive degrees from a vocational school in three years, but if they want to go to college they must spend four years studying at the gymnasium.

Those who graduate from the gymnasiums or attend four years of vocational school can earn admission into one of Bosnia and Herzegovina's four universities. The universities in Bosnia and Herzegovina schedule their classes from October to July.

But war changes everything, and education is no exception. With the nation split into two ethnic entities, both the Federation and the RS established their own educational systems with their own curricula. National unity is impossible when the Federation and the RS are teaching their students different versions of national history, languages, and ethics.

Schools in both parts of the country tend to teach ethnic pride, which is not necessarily a bad thing. Yet according to one study of Bosnian education researched by a university in Austria, this has in many cases crossed the line from pride to racial and ethnic intolerance of others. Some just teach political untruths.

For example, some textbooks used in Bosnia and Herzegovina were written and published in Croatia and Yugoslavia and are slanted toward the Croatian and Yugoslavian versions of politics and history. Bosnian Croat children who read these textbooks are taught that their real president is not the president of Bosnia and Herzegovina but that of the nation of Croatia. Similarly, some Bosnian Serbs learn that the RS should be recognized as its own state and not as part of the nation of Bosnia and Herzegovina. The Austrian university study also reported that textbooks used in Bosnian classrooms frequently blame other ethnic groups for being the aggressors in the Bosnian War and for committing war crimes.

Nonetheless, the region has had a tradition of quality higher education dating back centuries, just like most of western Europe. It can be traced to 1531 when an academy called the Hanikah was established in Sarajevo by an educator named Gazi Husrev-beg. Originally a place to study philosophy, the Hanikah added a separate school for the study of Islamic sciences in 1537. For centuries students came here to learn about and debate issues of philosophy, theology, and law.

The modern history of higher education in Bosnia and Herzegovina dates to 1949, when the University of Sarajevo was founded. The largest of Bosnia's universities, it began with five separate colleges devoted to medicine, law, teacher training, agriculture, and engineering. Within three years colleges of philosophy and economics were added. Today the university has more than two dozen colleges including those devoted to music, criminal science, three kinds of engineering (civil, mechanical, and electric), and veterinary medicine. Thanks to the fortitude of the students, teachers, and administration, the University of Sarajevo operated throughout the three and a half year siege of Sarajevo.

The country's three other universities are those of Banja Luka, Tuzla, and Mostar, founded in rapid succession respectively in 1975, 1976, and 1977. These three universities have strong emphases on the sciences, with colleges in subjects such as medicine, mechanical and electrical engineering, forestry, and mining. However, in 1999 the University of Banja Luka expanded beyond scientific study when it opened its Academy of Arts. The University of Tuzla, meanwhile, boasts an Academy of Drama.

Prior to the war, there was a hefty mix of Bosniaks, Croats, and Serbs teaching and taking courses in the nation's four universities. That diversity has lessened since the war ended.

In the wake of the war, a few specialty schools have been started. On October 5, 1998, the School of Journalism in Sarajevo officially opened. It is a completely independent school having nothing to do with the government of Bosnia and Herzegovina. It was established with the financial support of the European Commission in Brussels, Belgium, and the government of France, and with the professional support of a French educational facility, the Journalism School of Lille, and an organization called Media Plan. This journalism school is the first of its kind in Bosnia; it offers journalism students a nine-month general program with laboratory work involving newspapers, radio, television, or the Internet.

A Media Plan spokesperson emphasized at the time the importance of the Bosnian school. "Journalism education is a strategic issue for the further development and democratization of Bosnian media. The ranks of Bosnian media staff have been reduced to half their pre-war size."

A little less than a year earlier some of the music world's biggest names came out in force for the opening of another specialty school, this one in Mostar. Bono, the lead singer for U2, Bianca Jagger, rock music producer and performer Brian Eno, and the Irish Celtic-rock group The Chieftains were on hand to celebrate the opening of the Luciano Pavarotti Music Center, named in honor of the famed Italian opera singer. Upon arriving they were serenaded by choruses of Muslim, Croat, and Serb children rendering a song locally popular: "When You're Happy."

Built on the site of a primary school virtually destroyed by bombs during the war, the center is a multifunctional facility devoted to all types of learning with and through music. This includes basic music lessons, music therapy, music workshops, recording studios, and performance areas. Music therapy is an unusual offering in many music schools, but it was included in the Pavarotti Center to help children who had been traumatized by nearly four years living with bombs, death, and destruction. At the opening ceremony, Pavarotti exclaimed to the gathered crowd, "In 1995 we were looking for something to do for the benefit of kids. Today here we are where a dream is coming true." To the assembled children, he cautioned, "You saw the horror of war. Try to maintain peace when you grow up."

Refugees

One of the most troubling and continuing aspects of daily life here has been the refugee situation. Even though it has been many years since the Dayton Peace Agreement, native Bosnians who left their homeland during the fighting are still in the process of returning home.

From the end of the war through the end of 2001, more than 388,000 refugees returned to their Bosnian homes, yet about 650,000 were still displaced. A little over two-thirds of those uprooted were living in other parts of Bosnia, while less than one-third were in foreign countries, mostly Sweden and Germany. Roughly 232,000 were in the RS while about 210,000 were residing in the Federation.

The number of refugees returning peaked in 1997, when 120,000 moved back home. That number has decreased dramatically, with 18,700 persons returning to Bosnia in 2001. Many of those returning from other countries find themselves homeless since some other displaced persons now occupy their homes. Those internally displaced people are forced to live with extended family or acquaintances. Others, usually the elderly, poor, or disabled find homes in collective centers.

On a positive note, ethnic minorities in the Republic Srpska and the Federation have been returning to their original residences. One reason is that they have been encouraged by the UN Office of the High Representative, which has been enforcing Bosnia's property laws that help people return to their legally owned property. In December 2001, the High Representative amended existing Bosnian property laws even more by restricting the right to alternative accommodations to only the most vulnerable cases. Then again, another factor in the return of ethnic minorities has been the relative peace in the region since the war's end. The presence of the NATO troops has added to those feelings of security.

This is not to say that returning minorities have had an easy time. (Most tend to be rural rather than urban residents, since there are fewer chances for confrontations with the majority population.) Those returning to city homes face numerous problems. They commonly have trouble finding work because of both the stagnant economy and ethnic discrimination. According to the UN High Commissioner for Refugees (UNHCR), reconstructing has been slowed by a lack of international funds. The poor quality of education for minorities, especially in the RS, where the school system is known for teaching biased versions of the Bosnian War, has deterred returnees. According to a UNHCR survey taken in 2001, 85 percent of minority schoolchildren living in the RS attend school in the Federation.

Finally, despite the presence of NATO troops, there is always a threat of violence in this area where emotions run high. In the early 2000s, a

78-year-old Muslim man in the Serb-dominated town of Pale was hacked to death, and a 16-year-old Muslim girl was shot in her home, in the village of Piskavica, about 30 miles from Srebrenica.

It was in April 2001 when the first significant large group of Muslims briefly returned to Srebrenica since the July 1995 massacre. The United Nations praised the return as a huge step toward the rebuilding of Bosnia as a multicultural society. A 51-year-old Muslim woman, Hajra Ademović, on the verge of tears, recalled the Srebrenica massacre. "I lost three sons, three grandsons and most of the rest of my male family that July. But I do want to return here. Only here is my home where I can live with my memories of my beloved ones."

Food

People go hungry during any war, and they certainly did during the Bosnian War. But when times are good, Bosnians love to eat. With three generations often living under one roof, meals are a true family affair and food shopping is done on a regular, sometimes daily, basis.

Bosnians, like Americans, eat three traditional meals a day, but not according to the same pattern and not with the same foods as Americans. Bosnian cuisine has been greatly influenced by living hundreds of years under Turkish rule. Lamb, beef, baklava, and pita bread are staples.

At a Bosnian meal Americans will find many things they consider weird, such as hot dogs for breakfast. But with or without that ballpark specialty at their morning meal, breakfast is usually filling. Expect to find scrambled eggs, cheese, bread with honey, jam, or butter, with tea or warm milk to wash it down.

Lunch, not supper, is the big meal of the day, and it is not eaten until four o'clock in the afternoon. It might begin with a bowl of soup and continue with a favored regional concoction like Bosnian hotpot stew, known locally as *bosanski Ionac*. This is a layered dish including cabbage and other vegetables and four different types of meat, and it is traditionally served in a ceramic pot that has a strong resemblance to a flower vase.

When not chowing down on *bosanski Ionac*, Bosnians might be indulging all sorts of favored regional foods, such as:

1. *ćevapčići*, a 400-year-old dish that is a kind of kebab consisting of beef and lamb rolls surrounded by a squishy bread called *somun*
2. *burek*, a layered meat pie but without the vegetables found in *bosanski Ionac*
3. a cheese pie called *sirnica* or a spinach pie known as *zekjanica*
4. pita, which refers not only to a type of flat bread, but also baked dough filled with cheese, meat, spinach, and a starchy vegetable like pumpkin or potato
5. for those with strong stomachs, there is *sogandolma,* an onion stuffed with meat and rice

An everyday lunch will likely be followed by a dessert such as pudding, fruit, or cake. Dessert might be baklava, which is chopped nuts and honey baked in thin, light, and airy pastry, or something heavier like *tufahije,* apple cake with walnuts and dollops of whipped cream on top served on a special occasion or holiday. While the adults relax after dinner with coffee, the kids will have milk or soft drinks. The third meal, supper, is eaten late, around eight o'clock in the evening and because lunch was consumed just four hours earlier, is usually more of a snack than a meal.

Men and women tend to prefer different drinks in Bosnia. Women gravitate toward locally concocted fruit juices, while men favor regionally made brandies, like plum brandy called *šljivovica,* or grape brandy called *loza.* Also generally available is a yogurt drink called *kefir,* a specially brewed Bosnian tea called *salep,* strong Turkish and Italian coffees, and Coca-Cola, which is as common here as in much of the world. Bosnians typically socialize over several hot cups of strong coffee.

Most Bosnians would rather eat meals at home and reserve their evening out for drinking coffee. Those who do eat out can take a seat at an *aščhinica,* an East European– or Turkish-style restaurant where regional dishes including kebabs, meat pies, salads, and baklava are served. One of the most famous in Sarajevo is Hadžibajrić's, which has been in business for many generations and is known for preparing its food once a day, in the morning. When every last crumb of what the chef has prepared is gone, Hadžibajrić's closes for the day.

Ethnic restaurants can be found, too, including those serving Chinese, Indian, and different types of American food. Sarajevo even boasts a restaurant called Texas, serving burritos and other Texas-style Mexican foods. Pizzerias are common, but they do not serve pepperoni and mushroom slices. Bosnian pizzas are usually topped with dried meat and come with a cooked egg in the middle. And do not use your hands; Bosnians eat their pizza with a knife and fork.

Fast food restaurants are found on city streets here as elsewhere, but again, the menu is very different from what is served in America. Instead of cheeseburgers and French fries, *ćevapčići* is the most commonly served food at Bosnian fast food emporia.

Family and Leisure

Bosnians—in spite of all they have suffered—love to laugh. They are well known in eastern Europe for their wonderful sense of humor. One might even say they have gotten by on their humor, and their admirable ability to laugh at themselves. One man who moved from Sarajevo to the country of Slovenia, also a former Yugoslav republic, told a travel writer, "Slovenians and Bosnians have a lot in common—you like to make fun of Bosnians and so do we."

Bosnians are also known for having close-knit families, which explains their readiness to live among three generations in one house. In Bosnia, divorces and nursing homes are much less common than other countries. At times, housing shortages have forced divorced couples to live in the same house or apartment by necessity rather than choice. The elderly are mostly watched over by younger family members, while friends and relatives assist young parents by helping take care of their small children.

Unlike the majority of Muslim countries, women today have equal rights in Bosnia and Herzegovina. In the cities, most work outside the home in the same occupations as men. But as in many Western nations, equal rights outside the home does not translate into the same at home. Women in Bosnia still take care of most traditional women's jobs at home, such as cleaning, cooking, and shopping.

What do most Bosnians do for an evening out? Adults may head to a jazz club or pub in a city, but most of the time would just as soon get together with friends or coworkers for an evening of dancing, chatting, or playing games such as Yahtzee, chess, and cards. Rock is the music of youth and rebellion here as in North America and western Europe. Teenagers attend live rock concerts in the thousands. They might also spend an evening at a friend's house or socializing at a café. Country people do not have quite as much leisure time as urban dwellers. Summer is planting season and rural residents are often out well into the long summer nights tending to their crops.

Dress

Have a seat outdoors in any city or town in Bosnia and Herzegovina, whether it be Sarajevo or a smaller municipality such as Tuzla, and watch the passers-by. You will likely see hordes of people dressed in a kind of national uniform: blue jeans and T-shirts. Of course, that is no different than in most cities in the West. No one wears national folk dress for comfort.

But dressing so casually is a fairly new thing here. It was not much more than a generation ago that Bosnians could be seen on the streets in all sorts of folk outfits. Men in cities wore a fez, a vest over a striped shirt, a cummerbund, or broad sash around the waist, and breeches. Women living in the mountains wore baggy trousers called *dimije*, which date from the Ottoman Empire. *Dimije* were usually worn in different colors, depending on which folk group the women belonged to. People would say one could tell how high the snow was in the mountains by how high a woman tied her *dimije* around her ankles to keep them out of the snow.

The places one can most likely see such costumes today are folk fairs. However, now and then an older man in a city will be dressed in breeches and striped shirt, or a woman in a small mountain village will be wearing *dimije*.

Something not seen here, which is commonplace in the majority of Muslim countries, is the purdah, the tent-like covering worn by women to conceal their entire bodies, from head to toe. Purdahs never caught on among the Muslim women in Bosnia, although on religious holidays some Muslim women may wear a modern-day version of the purdah: a long raincoat and a headscarf. One-time president of Bosnia and Herzegovina, Alija Izetbegović, when accused of using the tenets of Islam as a basis for the laws in Bosnia, said, "We are not creating an Islamic state here. There are women with scarves, but in short skirts as well."

Holidays

If you would like to find a place where the holidays never seem to end, head to Bosnia and Herzegovina. Thanks to the many cultures here, the Bosnian calendar lists as many as 30 holidays per year. Many are religious in nature, while some are secular. Some are celebrated by all residents, some by just a select group.

Spring, for example, is a big time for religious holidays. Croatian Catholics and Eastern Orthodox celebrate Easter on different days, but both groups enjoy the holiday by decorating eggs and visiting with friends. Bosnian Jews, like Jews everywhere, have Passover in spring; it is an eight-day long holiday, in which they commemorate the biblical exodus from Egypt. It begins with a long and leisurely festive meal called a seder on the first, and sometimes the second night.

Bosnian Muslims attend prayers during the festival of Eid at the Gazi-Husrev Beg Mosque in Sarajevo on December 5, 2002. Eid marks the end of the holy month of Ramadan, during which Muslims fast from dawn to dusk. (AP/Wide World Photos/Sava Radovanovic)

Similarly, Bosnian Christians observe Christmas on different days. Catholics have Christmas on December 25 and usually wait until Christmas Eve to decorate their trees. The Eastern Orthodox Christmas is January 7. An early winter holiday for Jews is Hanukkah, an eight-day-long event in which Jews recall the Maccabees' victory over the Syrians in 165 B.C. The other major holidays for Jews are Rosh Hashanah, the Jewish New Year, and Yom Kippur, the Day of Atonement, both early fall celebrations. Jews, Eastern Orthodox, and Catholics also have several minor holidays on their calendar every year.

For Bosnian Muslims, the biggest religious holiday lasts a month and is called Ramadan. It takes place during the ninth month of the Muslim calendar and is a time for worship and contemplation. Muslims fast during daylight hours during the entire month, eating small meals with friends and family after dark. During Ramadan's last three days, known as Bajram, Muslims exchange small gifts. The minarets, or towers attached to mosques, are lit with strings of electric lights.

One of the biggest secular holiday celebrations in Bosnia is New Year's Day. Children place wish lists under their pillows a few nights earlier and receive presents, on New Year's Eve. People entertain one another with house parties and at midnight the skies are illuminated with the raucous sounds and glaring colors of fireworks. Other important secular national holidays are National Independence Day on March 1, Labor Day on May 1, and Bosnia-Herzegovina Day, also known as National Day, on November 25.

Sports and Recreation

Soccer, as in all of Europe, is the national sport here, but Bosnians have also fallen in love with the purely American sport of basketball. Over the last couple of decades Bosnians have spent a lot of time watching the sport and playing it. Bosnia has a national team, and also its own Bosnian League. A basketball club called Play Off was founded in Sarajevo in May 1998 for children of all ages, and has been going strong ever since.

In the spring of 2001, the U.S. Embassy in Sarajevo made an effort at diplomacy through basketball. The United States, with private companies Coca-Cola and Austrian Airlines, sponsored a series of basketball

Team Bosnian soccer player Saša Papac (right) dribbles the ball downfield in a match against Team Germany in October 2002. Soccer is by far the most popular sport in Bosnia and Herzegovina. (AP/Wide World Photos/Amel Emric)

clinics for all Bosnian children in Sarajevo, Banja Luka, and Tuzla. The clinics were led by Don Casey, former NBA head coach of the New Jersey Nets and Los Angeles Clippers. In addition, Casey went out of his way to appear with local sports celebrities at orphanages in each of the participating cities.

When not indoors on the court, Bosnians spend their summers swimming and fishing at lakes or strolling on the salt water beaches of the Adriatic Sea. Those staying overnight might rent a campsite or cabin, or perhaps stay at cottages they own. Ones who would rather not rough it have the option of hotels and company-sponsored resorts. They also enjoy hiking the many mountains, or spreading out a tablecloth for a relaxing picnic in the countryside. In winter, they take advantage of the mountains, too, savoring a day of quality sledding or skiing on some of Europe's steepest slopes.

NOTES

p. 109 "Most of the people . . ." "Reconstruction of Bosnia and Herzegovina: Housing in Bosnia before the War," World Bank website. Available on-line. URL: http://www.worldbank.org/html/extdr/extme/housing2.htm. Downloaded October 1, 2002.

p. 109 "It has been estimated that . . ." "Reconstruction of Bosnia and Herzegovina: Housing in Bosnia before the War."

p. 109 "Of those, about 18 percent . . ." "Reconstruction of Bosnia and Herzegovina: Housing in Bosnia before the War."

p. 109 "Sarajevo alone, a city of 374,000 . . ." Huremovic Mehmedalija, "The Current Status of Tenants in Bosnia-Herzegovina." Available on-line. URL: http:www.sllist.ba/Aktuelno/Page . . . Downloaded October 1, 2002.

p. 111 "Schools in both parts of the country . . ." Christof Bender, "Country Reports on Education: Bosnia and Herzegovina," Karl-Franzens-Universität Graz website. Available on-line. URL: http://www=gewi.kfunigraz.ac.at/csbsc/documentary-report/Bosnia.html. Downloaded October 1, 2002.

p. 113 "'Journalism education is a strategic issue . . .'" "A New School of Journalism in Sarajevo," International Journalists' Network website. October 8, 1998. Available on-line. URL: http://www.ijnet.org/Archive/1998/10/8-5180.html. Downloaded September 30, 2002.

p. 113 "'In 1995 we were looking for something . . .'" "The Opening of the Pavarotti Music Center," War Child Bulletin 4, December 21, 1997. Available on-line. URL: http://www.warchild.org/news/bull4/muscntr.html. Downloaded September 26, 2002.

p. 114 "From the end of the war . . ." "Country Report, 2002," U.S. Committee for Refugees home page. Available on-line. URL: http://www.refugees.org/world/countryrpt/europe/2002/bosnia_herce.htm. Downloaded January 9, 2003.

p. 114 "Roughly 232,000 . . ." "Country Report, 2002."

p. 114 "The number of refugees . . ." "Country Report, 2002."

p. 114 "According to the UN High Commissioner for Refugees . . ." "Country Report, 2002."

p. 115 "'I lost three sons . . .'" "Srebrenica Refugees Return," April 27, 2001. Available on-line. URL: http://news.bbc.co.uk/1/low/world/europe/1299581.stm. Downloaded September 8, 2003.

p. 117 "'Slovenians and Bosnians . . .'" "Cultural Tips," Virtual Tourist home page. Available on-line. URL: http://www.virtualtourist.com/m/.137577/151/?s+K&TID+10. Downloaded November 20, 2001.

p. 118 "'We are not creating . . .'" "Bosnian Serbs Drop Secession Demands, but New Splits Emerge," CNN website, September 19, 1996. Available on-line. URL: http://www.cnn.com/WORLD/9609/19/bosnia.elex. Downloaded September 23, 2002.

9
CITIES

The cities of Bosnia and Herzegovina have been bombed, burned, looted, and plundered. Yet they survive. They show their scars from the most recent war, but for the last several years they've attempted to ease back into some kind of normality.

Sarajevo

With a population of 374,000, the nation's colorful capital is located in east-central Bosnia, in the Federation on the border of the Republika Srpska. Sarajevo was once one of the most exciting and exotic cities in the world and has been called everything from the Jerusalem of Europe to Europe's most Oriental, or Eastern, city. Four religious groups and numerous ethnicities have lived here side by side for hundreds of years. The sizzle of meat being grilled in an open market, the peal of the bells from a Catholic church, the wailing call to worship from atop a minaret, and rock music blasting from inside a café can be heard simultaneously by anyone walking the city's streets.

For nearly four years those carefree sounds were replaced by the blasting of gunfire and rockets. Thousands of residents left and many have not returned. More than 10,500 citizens of Sarajevo died during the Bosnian War, and another 50,000 were injured. There are still damaged buildings and other visual reminders of the war in the streets.

Today street trams are running once more and most of the cafés, marketplaces, and other businesses have reopened. Still, things are not the same. For example, miles of new graveyards stretch alongside Koševo Stadium in Sarajevo—these did not exist before the war.

People have lived in Sarajevo for thousands of years, long before it was a city. Tools and weapons discovered by archaeologists near the Sarajevo airport have been dated to 2000 B.C. The oldest architecture dates from the Ottoman period and includes the Gazi Husrev-beg Mosque, built around 1531, and Morica Han, a Turkish-style inn built in the late 1590s when Sarajevo was on a major caravan route linking Europe and present-day Turkey.

Sarajevo's highly regarded museums draw as many visitors as do the historic landmarks. The National Museum is across the street from a Holiday Inn hotel that served as headquarters for foreign journalist covering the Bosnian War (which makes the hotel an historic landmark in its own right). For a while, the museum served as home to the parliament of Bosnia and Herzegovina while the country was getting back on its feet. Now it is open part time to those who want to see its collections, which include age-old relics like Greek and Roman tombstones, and medieval artifacts such as swords and coins.

Surrounding the National Museum are a botanical garden, Sarajevo's Museum of Natural History, and its Ethnography Museum, where centuries worth of local fashion and design are on view. It is not as boring as it sounds; one re-created historic scene shows a boy and a girl on a date centuries ago. The boy is sitting outdoors by the house's latticework, playing his sitar; the girl stays inside the house and, with the approval of her parents, listens to his personal performance.

One of the city's newest museums is a highly unusual one: a house that belonged to a family named Kolar that lived near a runway at the Sarajevo airport. With Sarajevo under siege during the Bosnian War, there was no way to get food and other supplies to the city's residents. The Bosnian army came up with an ingenious idea: a tunnel. The Kolar family donated their house to the army and it served as the tunnel's starting point. After seven months of digging, the tunnel connected the city with the outside world until the war was complete. People and provisions were transported back and forth through the tunnel. Today the Kolar House is the Tunnel Museum, with exhibits about the tunnel project, and even a small portion of the tunnel visitors can walk into.

Then again, just a short walk from these eternal landmarks in downtown Sarajevo is the city's premier disco club, the Senator, open nights for dancing and meeting people. The Senator is a true blending of West and East and proof that life goes on.

Banja Luka

This city of 220,000 residents in north-central Bosnia is the capital of the Republika Srpska. Banja Luka is to Bosnia Serbs what Sarajevo is to the country as a whole: their political, business, and cultural center. It was a focal point of Serb nationalism during the Bosnian War. During those years the Serbian military, with the cooperation of local Serbs, destroyed all 16 of the city's mosques. Today it is inundated with Serbian refugees from the rest of Bosnia. And while it is politically a part of the nation of Bosnia and Herzegovina, its businesses and economic structure has much closer ties to the republic of Serbia in the current Yugoslavia.

What human beings destroyed in the 1990s, nature took care of in 1969. A disastrous earthquake ravaged much of the town and surrounding area. It took years, but many new buildings were constructed to replace those ruined by the quake.

Partly because of the number of new structures, Banja Luka is not a tourist attraction like spirited Sarajevo. Vacationers will journey here to visit the countryside around Banja Luka. It sits in a valley surrounded by a blanket of mountain greenery.

Though evidence of Banja Luka's past has been destroyed, it has a long history. Thanks to archaeological digs, researchers have learned that early tribes lived here as early as the first century A.D.

Mostar

The center of the Federation community of Mostar in southwestern Bosnia and Herzegovina is an exquisite example of a medieval town, and looks like a setting of one of Grimm's fairy tales. The oldest part of town, known as Kujundžiluk, is dotted with cobblestone streets and packed with houses with reddish, angled roofs. Minarets once pierced the skyline while the jagged peaks of the mountains of Herzegovina encircle the city. Unfortunately, many minarets disappeared when several mosques were demolished during the war.

Before the war, Mostar had a population of 132,000, with sizable portions of Bosniaks, Croats, and Serbs. Today the population is down to 60,000 people, and virtually no Serbs remain here. The Muslims and Croats remain segregated, with Muslims living on the eastern side of the Neretva River, which was badly damaged during the war, and Croats living on the less marred western side. There is also a deep mistrust between the two groups. While some Muslims and Croats are attempting to bridge the two sides, there are observers who say that rabble-rousing politicians and persons involved in organized crime are doing their best to stop any conciliation from occurring.

Bridging the two sides is a literal as well as figurative idea in Mostar. The very name of the town means "old bridge" and when the famous centuries-old Ottoman-era bridge was destroyed it left a hole in the hearts of both the people who live here and those who have visited and fallen in love with the town. The old bridge has been replaced by a temporary metal, swinging one, since it is hoped that some day a stone bridge similar to the original one will span the Neretva River once more.

Tuzla

The commercial, cultural, and educational center of northeast Bosnia, Tuzla is located in the Federation, near the RS border. It is the fourth biggest city in the nation with a population of about 100,000. For a mid-size city, Tuzla has many cultural institutions including a well-regarded theater, several museums, an historic archive, and other arts centers. It also ranks second to Sarajevo in terms of educational facilities, with 22 full-time primary schools, two special needs schools, and a primary music school.

But what many come to Tuzla for are the works of nature as opposed to those of humankind. Tuzla is home to warm, therapeutic salt water springs, and they have long been exploited for the sake of people's health.

With a water temperature of 27.7 degrees Celsius (about 85 degrees Fahrenheit), the springs are healing and soothing for people whose muscles ache or who simply need to relax.

Records show that people have been coming to soak in Tuzla's salt water springs for over 1,000 years. A Byzantine historian named Constantine Porfirogenet mentioned the existence of the springs in his writings around the year 950. At that time, present-day Tuzla was called Salines, from the Latin word *salinus* meaning "salt." Similarly, the root of Tuzla, *tuz*, is the Turkish word for salt.

When people in Tuzla were not soaking in salt, they were processing it. Salt production has been one of the city's biggest industries for a long time. Tuzla's Museum of Technical Culture was once a *solana,* or old salt-making factory. But there is a downside to exploiting this natural resource. Mining—of salt and other mineral resources—has caused the terrain to sink as much as 10 meters, or more than 30 feet. Because of this, many Tuzla landmarks, including old buildings in historic areas, have had to be razed. There has been a movement in recent years to revitalize these neighborhoods.

Tuzla did not escape the war's wrath. A marker near an historic area known as Kapija, or "the gate," remembers the Tuzla citizens, many of them children, who were killed by a shell attack on May 25, 1995.

Brčko

When the details of the Dayton Peace Agreement were being finalized in 1995, the border city of Brčko was the odd man out. Brčko, with about 90,000 residents, sits on the border of Bosnia and Herzegovina and Croatia. More important, it also straddles the border of the Federation and the Republika Srpska. Located about 75 miles north of Sarajevo, Brčko is a key river port and railroad junction that links the Federation to western Europe.

But at the same time it straddles the narrow point connecting both eastern and western portions of the RS. Both the Federation and the RS insisted that Brčko must be part of their respective entities in Bosnia and Herzegovina. Who should govern Brčko was likely the most emotional issue being discussed in Dayton. Rather than have Brčko's status hold up the signing of a treaty ending a war filled with carnage of all varieties, the decision of what to do with Brčko was tabled for a later date.

A year before the war began, Serbs accounted for only 21 percent of Brčko's residents. On the other hand, Bosniaks comprised 44 percent and Croats made up 25 percent of the population. Then in 1992, the Yugoslav army in conjunction with Serb militias took control of the town and began ethnic cleansing. Bosniaks and Croats were forcibly removed from the city, and it is estimated that 3,000 Brčko residents who were not of Serbian ethnicity were murdered.

The Serbs insisted Brčko was rightly theirs since they were entitled to an uninterrupted path between both sections of the RS. Bosniaks said that allowing the Serbs to keep Brčko would be equivalent to rewarding them for their war atrocities. Finally, on March 5, 1999, nearly three and a half years after Dayton, officials from the North Atlantic Treaty Organization decided to turn Brčko into a neutral district governed by representatives of all three of Bosnia's ethnic groups. The Brčko District Statute was formally enacted on March 8, 2000.

Brčko's economic strengths have always been its agriculture and food production businesses. Favorable climate and soil conditions in and around the municipality allow farmers to grow everything from corn and wheat to fruits, vegetables, and herbs. A good number of dairy and livestock farms exist, as well as farms specializing in less common types of agriculture such as bee keeping. At one time corn covered about half of the arable land near Brčko. But during Bosnia's conversion from stateowned to free market, the demand for grains has decreased greatly. International advisers have encouraged Brčko farmers to concentrate on growing fruits, vegetables, and produce other than grains.

A Few Other Cities

After Mostar, one of the best surviving medieval towns in southeastern Europe is Jajce, a centrally located municipality in the Federation, just south of the Republika Srpska border. Before the coming of the Ottomans, the hilly village of 15,000 was the seat of the Christian kings of Bosnia. During the darkest days of World War II, it served for a brief time as the capital of liberated Yugoslavia. The delegates to the second session of the

Antifascist Council for the National Liberation of Yugoslavia met here in 1943 and officially announced a new constitution, with Josep Broz Tito legally replacing King Peter II as the nation's rightful leader.

In 1992, Jajce was the scene of an outrageous act of ethnic cleansing when the Serbian militia forced 35,000 Muslims to leave the city. Today with its original walls surrounding the old town, cobblestone streets, and centuries-old houses, Jajce awaits sightseeing visitors once more.

Like Brčko, the city of Bijeljina in the northeastern nook of Bosnia and Herzegovina, has a prime location. With about 90,000 inhabitants, Bijeljina is the second largest city in the RS. It is located along the principal thoroughfare that connects the eastern and western ends of the republic and along the main byway to the republic of Serbia. Its closeness to Serbia, and its very fertile land, has helped Bijeljina to develop a fairly healthy economy. However, much of the prosperity comes from a black market and smuggling operations.

Before the Bosnian War, more than 30,000 of Bijeljina's citizens were Bosniaks. Again, because of ethnic cleansing from 1992 through 1995, most of the Bosniak population was expelled. Only about 2,700 Bosniaks remain.

Located in the southernmost section of the RS near the Croatian border is Trebinje, a city of 35,000. It was traditionally one of the more sophisticated municipalities is what is now the RS, with well-developed educational and economic systems and cultural attractions. Unfortunately, its location caused it to be a center of war activities with Croatia. During the war much of the area in and round Trebinje was mined, and many minefields were left behind. The war may be long over, but Trebinje proves that its effects still linger.

NOTES

p. 123 "More than 10,500 . . ." Kate Galbraith. "Bosnia-Hercegovina," *Mediterranean Europe*, (Oakland, Calif.: Lonely Planet Publications, 1999), p. 131.

p. 126 "It also ranks second . . ." "A Little about Tuzla," Project Bosnia 2002 website. Available on-line. URL: http://www.artreachfoundation.org/tuzla.htm. Downloaded October 3, 2002.

p. 127 "A Byzantine historian . . ." "History of Tuzla," Tuzla website. Available on-line. URL: http://www.hr/tuzla/english/history.html. Downloaded October 3, 2002.

p. 127 "Mining of salt . . ." "About Tuzla," Tuzla website. Available on-line. URL: http://www.hr/tuzla/english/tuzla.html. Downloaded November 29, 2001.

p. 128 "On the other hand, Bosniaks . . ." "Information on Brčko District," Office of the High Representative, August 28, 2001. Available on-line. URL: http://www.ohr.int/print/?content_id=5530. Downloaded September 18, 2002.

p. 128 "Bosniaks and Croats were forcibly removed . . ." Norman Cigar and Paul R. Williams, "Reward Serbs with the Town of Brčko? Don't Do It," Christian Science Monitor website, March 11, 1998. Available on-line. URL: http://www.csmonitor.com/durable/1998/03/11/opin/opin2.html. Downloaded October 4, 2002.

p. 129 "Before the Bosnian War, . . ." "Introduction," Bijeljina website. Available on-line. URL: http://bijeljina.cc/english/. Downloaded November 29, 2001.

10

PRESENT PROBLEMS AND FUTURE SOLUTIONS

The war has been over for several years. But while a peace treaty can force armies to stop fighting, it cannot force people to like each other. Nor can it force people to work with each other and be kind to each other.

However, things are not all negative. In fact, considering how bad the situation could have gotten in Bosnia and Herzegovina, one might even admit that the current circumstances here are much better than what anyone predicted.

What Is Going Right

There is now peace in the region. It might be an uneasy and hesitant peace, but shellings no longer take place.

Much credit has to be given to the tens of thousands of United Nations peacekeepers, and to the will of many peace-starved citizens here for keeping the armies of Yugoslavia, Bosnia, and Croatia from continuing to fight one another.

Many citizens, even those who have suffered intense personal pain and anguish, are proving wrong those nay-sayers who said the people here could never escape their past and accept their neighbors. One example is Rifik Begić, a Muslim from Srebrenica, the town where the massacre of up to

10,000 Muslims occurred in 1994. Begić lost his leg and witnessed 150 people being killed. In spite of all he has suffered, Begic is putting his energies toward bringing Muslims and Serbs together. It has not been easy. Yet Begić states, "War is behind us and we have to work too hard to change."

But things must change for life in Bosnia and Herzegovina to get better. Following are some of the problems facing the rebuilding country, and some potential solutions.

Rebuilding

How does one rebuild a land which has been devastated? Homes, schools, hospitals, and other public buildings were heavily damaged or completely destroyed. It is estimated that 40 percent of the nation's bridges and 35 percent of its roads were seriously damaged or destroyed. Sarajevo International Airport, Bosnia's biggest, was the site of fierce fighting and suffered much destruction. Damage to the country's key transportation system, its railways, has been estimated at $1 billion.

Railways, roads, and airplanes are the lifelines of any nation. Without them, products cannot get to businesses or markets and people cannot get to work. For example, houses were destroyed in huge numbers leaving much of the population homeless. But in order to construct more houses, people and building materials must have a means of getting to the housing sites. If there is no way to get them to the sites, there will be no houses.

Slowly but surely, the nation is being reconstructed. Many organizations including the World Bank and the European Bank for Reconstruction and Development (EBRD) have loaned millions of dollars to rebuild Bosnia and Herzegovina's transportation system and other segments of the nation's infrastructure.

Encouraged by the reconstruction efforts, an increasing number of refugees are returning to their former homes. In 2001 alone, more than 92,000 Bosniaks, Serbs, and Croats came back to live where they did before the war.

A United Nations official named Werner Blatter said this proves that "people themselves feel confident enough to take the difficult decision to return to their homes and rebuild their communities. . . ."

The flip side to this trend is that because of the economic difficulties, many Bosnians want to leave their country. A 2002 survey by the United

Nations Development Program showed that "62 percent of young Bosnians see no future and want to emigrate." The head of the United Nations mission to Bosnia, Jacques Klein, commented, "Their parents made terrible historical errors. They almost destroyed their own future, and mortgaged their children's very heavily."

Land Mines

The controversial use of land mines was practiced by the Yugoslav army during the war and although thousands have been cleared, it was estimated in June 2002 that more than 500,000 mines and other types of unexploded ammunition can still be found throughout Bosnia and Herzegovina, especially in the countryside.

On April 10, 2000, nearly five years after the war ended, the world's citizens were sickened to learn that three small children were killed when they accidentally wandered onto a minefield. So even though the fighting had officially ended, innocent people were still victimized by it. The International Red Cross stated in a 2002 fact sheet, "Bosnia and Herzegovina is one of the most mine-infested countries in the world. Mine clearance is extremely expensive and slow. It will be years, perhaps even decades, before mines no longer threaten people's lives."

Many organizations and foreign governments have been aiding Bosnia and Herzegovina by donating expertise and financial aid to mine clearance activities. By 2000, the United States alone had given more than $40 million to demining operations. The United States has also helped set up a mine clearance training school and three demining training centers.

Additionally, numerous humanitarian groups have assisted generously in the cause. The International Red Cross organized a mine awareness week in the RS and has held free programs to instruct citizens on how to take precautions to avoid mine-related accidents.

Economy

Even when it was a Yugoslav republic, Bosnia and Herzegovina's economy was weak. Between rebuilding after the war and changing from a socialist to a free-market business system, the general economy here continues to be feeble. If it was not for aid from other countries, the situation would be worse.

At the end of 2001, the per capita gross domestic product, or average annual income per person, was about $1,000. By contrast, the lowest median household income in the United States is in West Virginia where the average income was a little more than $35,000 per year.

If low wages were not enough of a problem to overcome, official government estimates put the unemployment rate at anywhere between 30 and 50 percent. Those who work in legitimate jobs often receive their pay months after it is due. Others are forced to work in sweatshops or other illegal enterprises, and they are paid even less money with few or no benefits, such as health and life insurance.

Some progress has been made in the banking and finance sectors of the economy, but the country has been slow to reach the same progress in changing from state-owned to private-owned businesses. Improvement, it is hoped, will come about in time, as the people get more and more used to a free-market economy.

Health

Despite Bosnia and Herzegovina's current status as one of Yugoslavia's poorest republics, before the war Sarajevo was home to some of the best hospitals in eastern Europe. That seemed to be all the more reason for the Yugoslavs to make them specific targets during the fighting. Most suffered great destruction.

Some hospitals have been rebuilt but there is still a lack of quality medical facilities. That is especially true outside Sarajevo. According to the U.S. State Department, "Private practitioners and dentists are becoming more common; however, quality of care varies and rarely meets U.S. or western European standards."

Again, aid from foreign nations and humanitarian groups has helped. The International Rescue Committee (IRC) launched a program to improve emergency obstetric care at three Bosnian hospitals. The IRC plans to accomplish this by training health care professionals and acquiring newer equipment and supplies. The IRC is also supporting a post-delivery family planning service. The program is being funded by the Bill and Melinda Gates Foundation.

Additional help came in the summer of 2002 from a Dutch medical group called the International Dialysis Center BV (IDC). The IDC donated millions of dollars to help build a state-of-the-art dialysis facility for people suffering from life-threatening kidney disease in Banja Luka. The results have been promising. One success story is 39-year-old Ljubimir Gajić, a father of two from Bijeljina. He commutes about 140 miles every other day to the new facility in Banja Luka. Ljubimir said that before, patients with various illnesses were grouped together, treatments lasted just two hours instead of the usual four, and the equipment was outdated. He added, "Treatment in Bijeljina was awful. We were treated only twice a week instead of every other day. I couldn't walk after treatment. I didn't have enough strength. Now I feel good."

Education

Rebuilding the numerous schools destroyed during four years of warfare is only one of the problems needing to be addressed. Other troubles relate to the lack of equipment—they need everything from computers to the most basic school things such as pens and pencils—or to the children themselves.

Some children, whose homes were destroyed, still move frequently. Many of those who do have stable homes deal with trauma—the effects of years of witnessing acts of violence. As a result they suffer flashbacks and have repeated nightmares. With such personal problems, it is understandable they have trouble concentrating in school. A lot of children act out aggressively, and perform poorly.

Again, help has come from outside Bosnia and Herzegovina, from other countries as well as international associations including the World Bank, the United Nations Educational, Scientific, and Cultural Organization (UNESCO), the Council of Europe, and the European Union. However, fixing a broken education system is not going to be cheap. The World Bank has said that $200 million will be needed to fully complete the job.

The first steps are reconstructing damaged schools, or creating entirely new ones. Then the infrastructure has to be rebuilt in order for the schools to have basic requirements such as electricity, water, and heat. Since many teachers still in Bosnia are volunteers who have never taken education classes, professional teachers have to be trained and money must be provided to pay them.

There are signs of hope. The ministers of education in both the Federation and the Republika Srpska signed an agreement on May 10, 2001, in which they declared they will make a real effort to check textbooks and curricula to make sure those used are not slanted or prejudiced in favor or against any of Bosnia's ethnic groups. In addition, the report stated that professional qualifications of teachers as well as students' assessments will be mutually recognized throughout Bosnia and Herzegovina. It further stressed that the country's colleges and universities will need to be more efficient and hold higher standards in their training of future teachers.

When the agreement was signed, Bosnia's Office of Human Rights released the following statement: "The children of Bosnia and Herzegovina are the future of Bosnia, and they must receive the best possible education. This means education which responds to the requirements of the present, education that will ensure employment, and education which will assist in creating a prosperous future for Bosnia and Herzegovina. Bosnia and Herzegovina needs education that is in accordance with European standards, and which instills in children a cosmopolitan and tolerant spirit and teaches them to think critically."

NOTES

p. 132 " 'War is behind us . . .' " Allen Pizzey, "Peaceful Coexistence Returning," CBS News website. Available on-line. URL: http://www.cbsnews.com/ stories/2001/04/08/world/printable284583.shtml. Downloaded September 14, 2002.

p. 132 "It is estimated that . . ." "The Story of Bosnia and Herzegovina." Available on-line. URL: http://bosniak.netfirms.com/research/bosnia.herzegovina.html. Downloaded August 31, 2002.

p. 132 "Sarajevo International Airport . . ." "The Story of Bosnia and Herzegovina."

p. 132 "In 2001 alone, . . ." "2001: The Highest Number of Returns Since Dayton," United Nations Refugee Agency press release. Available on-line. URL: http://www.unhcr.ba.

p. 132 "'people themselves feel confident . . .'" "2001: The Highest Number of Returns Since Dayton."

p. 133 "'62 percent of young Bosnians . . .'" "Bosnia: Ten Years After," originally published in *Bosnia Daily*, April 2, 2002, reprinted on ArtReach Foundation webpage under "Project Bosnia." Available on-line. URL: http://www.artreachfoundation.org/bosmain.htm. Downloaded October 3, 2002.

p. 133 "'Their parents made . . .'" "Bosnia: Ten Years After."

p. 133 "The controversial use of land mines . . ." "Bosnia and Herzegovina—Consular Information Sheet," U.S. State Department website, issued June 4, 2002. Available on-line. URL: http://travel.state.gov/bosnia-herzegovina.html. Downloaded October 4, 2002.

p. 133 "'Bosnia and Herzegovina is . . .'" "ICRC Activities in Bosnia-Herzegovina, January 2002," International Red Cross website. Available on-line. URL: http://www.icrc.org/. Downloaded October 8, 2002.

p. 133 "Many organizations and foreign governments . . ." "Text: U.S. Humanitarian Demining Assistance to Bosnia-Herzegovina," Washington File, U.S. State Department website. Available on-line. URL: http://usinfo.state.gov/topical/pol/arms/stories/00041803.htm. Downloaded October 8, 2002.

p. 134 "At the end of 2001, . . ." Bureau of Democracy, Human Rights, and Labor, U.S. State Department, "Bosnia and Herzegovina: Country Reports on Human Rights Practices—2001," dated March 4, 2002. Available on-line. URL: http://www.state.gov/g/drl/rls/hrrpt/2001/eur/8236.htm. Downloaded October 8, 2002.

p. 134 "By contrast, the lowest . . ." "Alaska Leads in Median Income," chart, *USA Today*, October 2002.

p. 134 "'Private practitioners . . .'" "Bosnia and Herzegovina—Consular Information Sheet," dated July 5, 2002. Available on-line. URL: http://travel.state.gov/bosnia-herzegovina.html. Downloaded October 4, 2002.

p. 135 "'Treatment in Bijeljina was awful . . .'" DevNews Media Center press release, "Revitalizing Bosnia-Herzegovina," dated July 29, 2002. Available on-line. URL: http://web.worldbank.org/WEBSITE/EXTERNAL/NEWS. Downloaded October 1, 2002.

p. 135 "Again, help has come from . . ." DevNews Media center press release, "Reconstruction of Bosnia's Education Immediate Policy," dated 2002. Available on-line. URL: http://web.worldbank.org/WEBSITE/EXTERNAL/NEWS. Downloaded October 1, 2002.

p. 136 "'The children of Bosnia and Herzegovina . . .'" Office of the High Representative Human Rights, Rule of Law Development, "Education Policy in Bosnia and Herzegovina," May 10, 2001. Available on-line. URL: http://www.ohr.int/print/?content_id=3519. Downloaded October 1, 2002.

CHRONOLOGY

1000 B.C.
First settlers migrate into what is now Bosnia

A.D. 9
Illyria becomes a Roman province called Illyricum

500s
Tribesmen known as Slavs enter region

600s
Other Slavic peoples, the Croats and Serbs gradually enter what is today
    modern-day Bosnia

700s
Franks conquer inhabitants of Bosnia; many forced to become Christians
    and serfs

1000s
Byzantine Empire conquers Bosnians

1137
Kingdom of Hungary overruns Byzantine Empire in Bosnia

1167
Byzantine Empire regains rule of Bosnians

1180
Hungary again beats Byzantines in Bosnia

1180–1204
Golden Age of Kulin Ban

1235–1241
Crusades against Bosnian Bogomils declared by Pope Innocent III

1308
Ban Stephan Kotromanić becomes ruler

1353
Ban Stephan Tvrtko becomes ruler

1389
Battle of Kosovo Polje on June 28

1465
Bosnia falls to Ottoman Turks

1481
Herzegovina falls to Ottoman Turks

1500s
City of Vrhbosna changes name to Sarajevo

1699
Treaty of Karlowitz gives Hapsburg Empire rule over most of Croatia, beginning of end of Ottoman Empire

1875
Christian Rebellion (Peasant Rebellion) takes place as Herzegovina Christians rebel against Muslim rulers

1878

Berlin Congress divides eastern Europe; Bosnia and Herzegovina put under *corpus separatum* rule of Kingdom of Austria-Hungary

1908

Austria-Hungary formally annexes Bosnia and Herzegovina

1912–1913

Balkan Wars

1914

Archduke Francis Ferdinand of Austria-Hungary assassinated in Sarajevo triggering World War I

1918

World War I ends; Serbian crown prince Alexander forms new nation: Kingdom of Serbs, Croats, and Slovenes

1921

Vidovdan Constitution, which recognizes Bosnia and Herzegovina's original borders, is approved

1929

Alexander names himself absolute ruler of the kingdom; old borders abolished and new ones drawn up; Alexander renames the country the Kingdom of Yugoslavia (Kingdom of the South Slavs)

1934

Alexander assassinated by member of ultra-nationalist Croatian group, Ustasha

1935

Milan Stojadinović named prime minister by Prince Pavle

1939

Dragiša Cvetković named prime minister by Prince Pavle

1941

Nazi Germany attacks Yugoslavia two years into World War II; Yugoslavia surrenders

1943

Antifascist Council for the National Liberation of Fascism, also known as the Partisans, meets in Jajce and makes plans for communist Josip Broz, Marshal Tito, to lead nation after the war

1945

Germany and Ustasha surrender to Yugoslav Partisans; World War II ends; Tito takes over nation's leadership, employs somewhat liberalized form of communist government referred to as Titoism; Bosnia and Herzegovina becomes a republic within Yugoslavia

1970s

Yugoslavia's economy weakens; people demonstrate in streets

1980

Tito dies; system of rotating presidents takes effect

1983

Krajgher Commission Report released, calls for some kind of free market economy in Yugoslavia

1984

Winter Olympics held in Sarajevo

1987

Agrokomerc scandal exposes widespread corruption in Yugoslavia

1989

Major unrest in nation with more than 1,900 labor strikes taking place

1990

January 23: The League of Communists in Yugoslavia dissolves
November: Alija Izetbegović of Muslim-dominated Party of Democratic Action (SDA) elected president of Bosnian republic

1991

June 25: Croatia and Slovenia declare independence from Yugoslavia; fighting begins between Croatia and Yugoslav army

1992

January 15: Bosnia and Herzegovina denied international recognition as a separate nation
February 29 and March 1: Referendum held in which Bosnia and Herzegovina votes for independence from Yugoslavia
April 6: United States and European Community recognize independent Bosnia-Herzegovina; war breaks out between Bosnia and Herzegovina and Yugoslavs
Summer: Sarajevo falls under siege
Early winter: UN declares several Bosnian cities as "safe areas."

1993

Spring: Bosnians and Croats fight over Mostar
May 25: United Nations War Crimes Tribunal established
November 9: Mostar bridge destroyed by Croatian soldiers

1994

February 5: Massacre of 68 civilians at market in Sarajevo
March: With help of United States, Croatia and Bosnia agree to form a Bosnia/Croat federation

1995

January 1: Four-month long truce between Bosnia's government and Bosnian Serbs is announced
February 23: UN War Crimes Tribunal charges 21 Bosnian Serbs with war crimes
July: Massacre at Srebrenica

October 5: Cease-fire announced for nearly all of Bosnia and Herzegovina

November 1: Peace talks begin at Wright-Patterson Air Force Base in Dayton, Ohio

November 21: Peace treaty agreed upon in Dayton ends Bosnian War

December 14: Peace treaty signed in Paris, France

1996

February 29: Bosnian government declares siege of Sarajevo officially lifted

May 31: Serb Dražen Erdemović, who took part in Srebrenica massacre, pleads guilty to murder; he is the first person convicted by International Criminal Tribunal, and is sentenced to 10 years in prison

1997

United Nations peacekeeping forces cut in half

1998

September 12–13: National elections held; moderate defeats nationalist for Serb seat in three-party presidency, but hard-liner Nikola Poplašen wins presidency of RS; nationalist wins Croat seat in presidency, Izetbegović wins Bosniak seat

2000

November 10: National elections held; nationalists win major victories

2001

Spring: Croat National Assembly declares self-rule; Croat leader Ante Jelavić removed from office by Office of the High Representative

2002

July 15: Presidents of Bosnia and Herzegovina, Croatia and Yugoslavia meet for first time since Dayton peace talks nearly seven years earlier

October 5: National elections held; nationalists win significant victories

FURTHER READING

Cataldi, Anna. *Letters from Sarajevo*. Translated by Avril Bardoni. Rockport, Md: Element Press, 1993.

Cothran, Helen. *War-Torn Bosnia*. San Diego: Greenhaven Press, 2001.

Dizdarevic, Zlatko. *Sarajevo: A War Journal*. Edited by Ammiel Alcalay; translated by Anselm Hollo. New York: Fromm International, 1993.

Donia, Robert J., and John V. A. Fine, Jr. *Bosnia and Hercegovina: A Tradition Betrayed*. New York: Columbia University Press, 1994.

Filipovic, Zlata. *Zlata's Diary: A Child's Life in Sarajevo*. New York: Viking Press, 1994.

Grant, James P. *I Dream of Peace: Images of War by Children of Former Yugoslavia*. New York: HarperCollins, 1994.

Malcolm, Noel. *Bosnia: A Short History*. New York: New York University Press, 1994.

O'Grady, Scott, with Michael French. *Basher Five-Two: The True Story of Fighter Pilot Captain Scott O'Grady*. New York: Doubleday, 1997.

Ousseimi, Maria. *Caught in the Crossfire: Growing Up in a War Zone*. New York: Walker & Co., 1995.

Reger, James P. *The Rebuilding of Bosnia*. San Diego: Lucent Books, 1997.

Ricchiardi, Sherry. *Bosnia: The Struggle for Peace*. Brookfield, Conn.: Millbrook Press, 1996.

Ricciuti, Edward. *War in Yugoslavia: The Breakup of a Nation*. Brookfield, Conn.: Millbrook Press, 1993.

Silverman, Robin Landew. *A Bosnian Family*. Minneapolis: Lerner Publications, 1997.

Simoen, Jan. *What About Anna?* New York: Walker & Co., 1999.

Tekavec, Valerie. *Teenage Refugees from Bosnia-Herzegovina Speak Out*. New York: Rosen Publishing Group, 1997.

Yancey, Dianne. *Life in War-Torn Bosnia*. San Diego: Lucent Books, 1996.

INDEX

949.742 SCH

Schuman, Michael.
Bosnia and Herzegovina.

DATE DUE

JUN - 7 2007		

GAYLORD   #3522PI   Printed in USA